Y0-AFX-622

# FUN WITH WOOD

*Books by Joseph Leeming:*

FUN WITH GREETING CARDS

FUN WITH ARTIFICIAL FLOWERS

FUN WITH SHELLS

FUN WITH WIRE

FUN WITH PENCIL AND PAPER

FUN WITH BEADS

FUN FOR YOUNG COLLECTORS

HOLIDAY CRAFT AND FUN

FUN WITH FABRICS

FUN WITH CLAY

FUN WITH MAGIC

FUN WITH WOOD

FUN WITH LEATHER

FUN WITH PAPER

FUN WITH BOXES

THE COSTUME BOOK FOR PARTIES AND PLAYS

FUN WITH PUZZLES

MORE FUN WITH MAGIC

PAPERCRAFT

# FUN WITH WOOD

## BY JOSEPH LEEMING

### ILLUSTRATED BY CHARLES E. PONT

How to whittle & carve wood
to make useful & decorative
articles, toys, puzzles, and
unusual figures

J. B. LIPPINCOTT COMPANY
PHILADELPHIA        NEW YORK

COPYRIGHT, 1942, BY JOSEPH LEEMING

All rights reserved. No part of this work may
be reproduced without the written
permission of the publisher.

*Eleventh Printing*

J 680
L5111

*Designed by*
CHARLES E. PONT

Library of Congress catalog card number 42-17492

Printed in the United States of America

FOR

MARION GILBERT

DEPOSIT LIBRARIES
66-176403

# FOREWORD

WHITTLING and wood carving are crafts that have given deep and enduring satisfaction to many thousands of people. They satisfy the urge to create, to make things that are interesting and beautiful, which every person feels.

You can start whittling with a pocketknife and a few spare bits of wood, and with this simple equipment and material you can make an endless number of amusing and ingenious toys and puzzles, or useful and decorative articles for use in your own home or to serve as gifts. As your skill increases, you can soon go on to whittling the intriguing animal and human figures which have been so popular in recent years. In these you can display your skill not only as a whittler, but as an artist, for you will gain skill in putting character and individuality into the faces and expressions of your figures.

Many people get their greatest thrill from making the standard master-pieces of the whittler's time-honored craft—a ball-in-a-cage, a wooden chain, or a graceful whittled fan. All these may be made from common-place bits of wood such as you see about you every day. But when the chain or ball-in-a-cage first emerges from the wood and begins to take its final shape, you really get "the thrill that comes once in a lifetime."

Wood carving may be considered as a pastime, or may be developed into an art as absorbing, as creative and as productive of beauty as painting or sculpture. Many of the great Greek sculptors worked in wood, as did Michelangelo, Donatello, and a host of other artists who are more widely known for their work in other forms of artistic creation. Probably the greatest of all woodcarvers was Grinling Gibbons, born in England in 1648, who executed commissions for Charles II, worked for Sir Christopher Wren, and did numerous carvings in Windsor Castle, Cambridge University, Canterbury Cathedral, and many other famous English churches. At one time Gibbons carved a pot of flowers over a doorway, which was so delicate that the flowers shook and nodded on their stems when coaches went by in the street. His talents were so renowned that George I appointed him his master carver in 1714.

We may not all become as skillful and famous as Grinling Gibbons, but we can share in the same joy of creating beautiful things that he obtained from wood carving. When starting in, all the equipment needed consists of three or four chisels or gouges, and a work bench or table. An endless number of carved pieces can be made with this simple equipment, and other tools may be added later if one wishes. The chief qualification for the beginner is the urge to make something. With this, and a little experimenting, you will soon be able to carve the many designs that are shown in this book.

In looking through the following pages, you will see many drawings of household articles and furnishings, such as bookends, picture frames, magazine holders, and wooden boxes, decorated by one or another form of carving. It should be noted, however, that while these objects are illustrated, the details of how to construct them are not gone into. In other words, this is not a book on carpentry. All the articles shown, and many more that can be decorated by wood carving, can be purchased inexpensively in an unpainted condition. Or, if you prefer to make your own, you will find descriptions of how to do so in the books listed in the bibliography given in the back of this volume.

JOSEPH LEEMING

# CONTENTS

## WHITTLING

## WHITTLED TOYS AND GAMES

## USEFUL GIFTS

## WHITTLED ANIMAL AND HUMAN FIGURES

## PUZZLES

## CHAINS AND INTERLOCKED RINGS

## CAGED BALLS AND RELATED FIGURES

## WHITTLED FAN FIGURES

## JOINTED FIGURES

## WOOD CARVING

## INCISED CARVING

# CONTENTS

## CARVING MODELED IN RELIEF

# WHITTLING

# WHITTLING

WHITTLING is probably the oldest form of wood carving, and it is without question one of the most fascinating. With a small or medium-sized pocket knife, you can make an almost endless number of puzzles, toys, games, human and animal figures, and other objects. If you have ever known an experienced whittler and have seen his work, you will know that an ordinary pocket knife can be a tool box in itself; that it can do practically everything that it is possible to do with an elaborate set of tools. The variety of ingenious and interesting articles that can be made by whittling, ranges from simple block puzzles and match-stick carvings to intricate wooden chains, elaborate fans, and life-like figures of human beings.

## KNIVES FOR WHITTLING

Many experienced whittlers use an ordinary pocket knife with two or three blades, such as can be purchased for about a dollar. The large heavy blade is used for rough cutting and the smaller blade or blades for fine work. It is best to get a good knife, so that you will be sure to have well tempered blades that will not lose their cutting edges. For some kinds of work, such as whittling a chain from a match stick, you will need a small knife with very thin blades; in other words, a special knife that will be suitable only for this exceptionally fine kind of work. Another knife with two large blades may also be found useful for such work as roughing out human or animal figures. For most purposes, however, the ordinary three-bladed knife will be all that you will need.

It is important that the knife blades be kept sharp. This cannot be overemphasized. More whittling has been spoiled by dull blades than by any other factor. When your blades commence to get dull, sharpen them at once, or your work will go poorly and the fun will go out of it.

A general rule for whittling is, "Whittle away from yourself," and it is wise to bear this in mind continually. In some cases, however, you will find that the rule has to be broken. If you have to whittle toward yourself, keep the hand holding the wood behind the knife blade. Furthermore, do not hold the wood against your stomach or your knee. Even the most careful worker sometimes makes a slip.

## WOOD FOR WHITTLING

Some of the best kinds of wood for whittling are soft white pine, yellow poplar, basswood, and straight-grained cedar. These woods are soft and usually split straight and evenly, and do not break open ahead of the knife blade. At the same time, they are strong enough to hold together even when whittled down to thin dimensions.

The small pieces of wood that are used for practically all whittling projects can be purchased very inexpensively from any lumber dealer or, in many instances, can be obtained from discarded wooden boxes. Ordinarily, most lumberjacks have at all times odd pieces of lumber that they sell at lower cost than the regular stock. Another good source from which to obtain wood consists of grocery, hardware, drug and department stores, as well as most other types of stores, which usually have a supply of wooden boxes they are glad to give away or sell for a few cents apiece. Many of these boxes are made of soft wood that has been planed to a smooth finish, and contain good straight-grained boards that are excellent for whittling. Use of sandpaper and a plane will remove markings stenciled on the boxes as well as scratches and other defacing marks.

As with anything else, once you start to look around for pieces of wood suitable for whittling, you will discover that they are all around you. There may be a plentiful supply, for example, in old boxes in your own cellar or attic or in those of your friends. Once you begin to look, moreover, you will find good boxes and good pieces of discarded lumber in the stores and in other places where they have been right along but have never come to your attention because you were not in need of them.

Fine woods, specially-cut pieces, and the numerous kinds of imported woods that are used by whittlers, carvers and cabinet makers can be purchased at surprisingly low prices from several firms that specialize in this field. The larger firms of this type advertise regularly in such magazines as "Popular Mechanics" and "Popular Science Monthly," and do most of their business by mail order with craftsmen situated in every part of the country. Their catalogs are fascinating and should be sent for by anyone who is interested in either whittling or wood carving.

## GRAIN

Everyone who whittles learns, after a very short period of experience, how to deal with the grain of wood to avoid splitting. Chiefly one can be guided by the application of plain commonsense to the obvious. That is, when one sees that the grain runs in such a way that it may split the wood, steps are taken to prevent such splitting.

Probably the principal thing to look out for is grain that twists or curves. Ordinary whittling in the direction of such grain may cause the wood to split along the grain. Assume, for example, that you are cutting out a silhouette and that the grain in the waste wood outside the figure's outline curves and passes into the wood of the figure itself. Careless whittling might easily make a cut that would extend along the curved grain, and so split the wood inside the figure. To prevent this, always "stop-cut" along the outlines of the figure. That is, hold the knife nearly perpendicular and draw its tip slowly along the outline, making a vertical cut. This stop-cut will sever the fibers of the wood and prevent splitting. This same principle can be applied to whittling other objects.

Another rule, when there is danger of the grain causing splitting, is to go slowly and make small cuts. Pare away small chips and thus keep the work and the grain under constant control.

Usually it is possible to whittle with the grain. When this is done, careful work and stop-cutting where needed will prevent splitting. The same rules apply, when you find it necessary to whittle against the grain. Here stop-cuts should be made to mark the line toward which you are whittling to keep the grain from carrying your cuts beyond that line. When you must whittle across a diagonal grain, care must be taken to keep the wood from splitting diagonally along the grain. Again, the rule is to whittle off small chips, instead of trying to cut off an entire section of waste wood with one sweeping cut. Also, divide the work into small sections by means of stop-cuts, and work on one section at a time.

A little experience is probably the best teacher where the handling of grain is concerned, but the principles just outlined should be of help to the beginner.

Silhouette figures for whittling

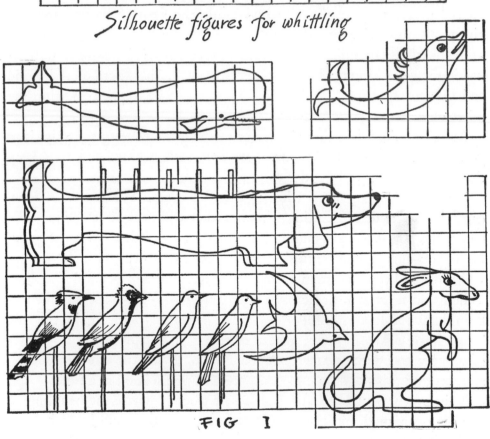

FIG I

## SILHOUETTE FIGURES

Silhouette figures are among the simplest objects made by whittling and are excellent to start with. Dozens of human and animal figures can be carved out of ¼-inch pine or other soft wood and, after being painted or enameled, can be used for garden ornaments, place cards, candle holders or other purposes that may suggest themselves. But it is not necessary by any means to turn these figures into useful articles. Simply put them on a mantel, bookcase or table, and the sight of them will bring pleasure. Or give them to the children to use as toys.

Fig. 1 shows a number of figures that can easily be whittled out of ¼- or ⅜-inch soft wood. First draw the figure on the wood. Then whittle out the outline, and mark in the interior lines with V-shaped grooves. Eyes and other indentations are made by using the tip of the knife blade.

The figures shown in Fig. 1 are drawn against a background of small squares, and are smaller than most carvers like their finished figures to be. To enlarge them, lay out ¼-inch or larger squares on the wood, and then copy in the outline of the figure square for square.

The birds shown in Fig. 1 may be brightly colored and mounted on pointed dowel sticks to serve as gay garden or lawn decorations. The dachshund has pieces of thin dowel mounted in holes drilled into his back, so that he can serve as a different kind of holder for spools of thread. To be sure that he will stand firmly, he should be made of wood

Fig 2

at least 1 inch thick. The child angel figures make intriguing Christmas tree decorations or can be glued to thin strips of wood to make candle holders. (Fig. 2.)

Other figures that will be amusing to whittle out can be found in magazines, children's books, and photographs. The Alice in Wonderland characters are enormously amusing—the Queen of Hearts, the Red Queen, the Mad Hatter, the White Knight, the Frog Footman, and all the others that have delighted thousands. Get a book with the original Tenniel drawings, and draw or trace the silhouette outlines of the figures. Then make a checker-board of squares of suitable size over the drawing. Draw another checker-board of similar or larger squares on the wood, and transfer the traced drawing, square by square, onto the wood.

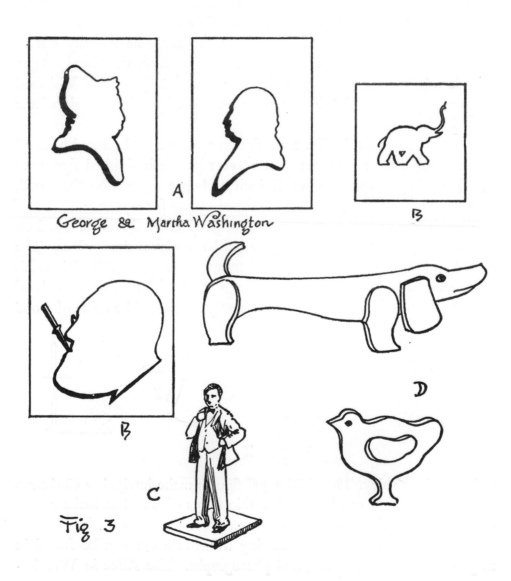

George & Martha Washington

Fig 3

Many such figures can be made with separate arms or legs. These are whittled out and are then fastened to the body by means of thin wires passed through holes drilled for the purpose. The ends of the wires are bent over and held securely in place by drops of glue or cement.

It may be noted here that silhouette figures can also be cut out with a jigsaw or coping saw. Some workers may prefer this quicker method, but born whittlers will stick to their pocket knives.

Fig. 3 shows some additional ways to use whittled silhouette figures. Profiles, like those of George and Martha Washington are easy to make. Simply trace the outline of their features from pictures in a history or other book; then transfer the tracing to ⅛-inch soft wood by using carbon paper. Cut out the silhouette by following the outline with the point of your knife blade. Finish the silhouette by sandpapering and waxing or shellacing it; and then mount the silhouettes on panels of walnut or some wood of contrasting color.

Silhouettes of many other famous people may be made in the same way, and make attractive gifts. You can also make silhouettes of this kind of your friends, by tracing profile views of their faces.

A different kind of silhouette work is shown at B in Fig. 3. Here the silhouettes are cut out of the panel. The space occupied by the face or other figure may be left open, or may be backed with parchment. If the latter is done, the finished silhouette should be hung where the light from a window or lamp will shine through the parchment. When making a silhouette of this kind, be careful not to force your knife through the grain or you will split the wood.

At C in Fig. 3 is shown a photograph mounted on a whittled-out wooden background. Figures of this kind made with photographs of yourself or your friends make interesting desk or table ornaments. The finished figure is glued to a wooden base so that it will stand upright.

Another way to treat cut-out silhouette figures is to emphasize certain parts by whittling them out separately and glueing them in place. Examples are the dachshund and bird shown at D, Fig. 3. The dachshund's legs and ears are whittled from separate pieces, as are the wings of the bird, and are then glued to the body.

## WHITTLED TOYS AND GAMES

AN ALMOST endless number of amusing or useful articles can be whittled out of wood, most of them so simple that even beginners will have no difficulty in making them. They are good practice for beginners, as a matter of fact, for their whittling furnishes good experience in handling a knife, dealing with the grain in the wood, and making the right kind of cuts, chiefly the small ones that are needed to avoid splitting the wood. Many beginners try to go ahead too fast and to shape up their projects with a few large cuts.

A little practice with the articles described in this section will soon give one a real and valuable working knowledge of the right speed with which to proceed to avoid spoiling the work by careless cutting. Practice on the simpler projects will also make much easier the later whittling of the classic masterpieces of the whittler's art, such as caged balls, chains and fans.

The articles described in this section should be regarded only as an indication of the great number of things that can be made and of the endless hours of "fun with wood" that anyone can enjoy. Suggestions for numerous other articles can be obtained by keeping your eyes open when visiting ten-cent stores, toy stores and department stores, and from illustrations and advertisements in magazines and newspapers.

All the figures illustrated may be painted in bright colors to add to their gaiety and attractiveness.

Fig. 1 shows some easy-to-make silhouette figures made into toys.

The hen and rooster are whittled out of ⅛-inch wood and each is firmly cemented to a piece of wood ¼ inch thick and 1 inch long. If preferred, the figures can be fastened to their base pieces with small brads for greater security. The two rails are of ⅛-inch wood, about ¼ inch wide and 4 inches long. The pan on the top rail is cut out in one piece with the rail itself. Fasten the pieces together with brads or cut-off pins, aligning the rails so that both figures stand upright when the ends of the upper and lower rails are in line. Now, by pushing the lower rail back and forth, the hen and rooster will alternately dip their beaks into the pan to gobble up the food.

At B, Fig. 1, is a chicken which lifts its head when its tail is pushed

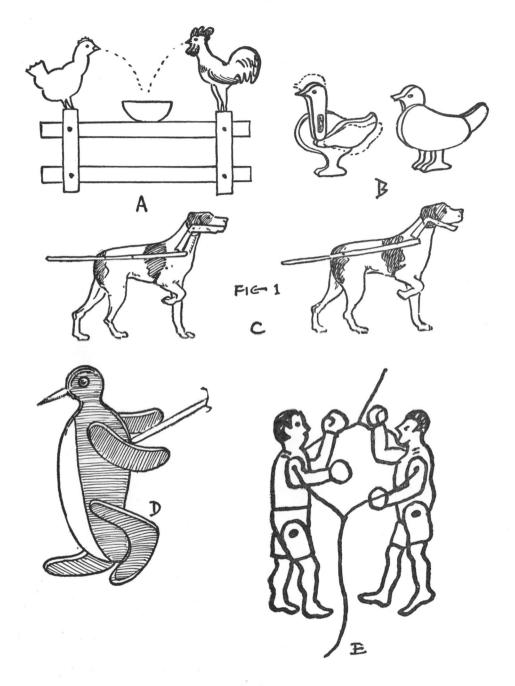

down, and at C, a spotted dog which opens its mouth to bark when its tail is moved. Both figures consist simply of whittled-out side pieces nailed together so as to enclose the two movable parts.

One of the most amusing, easy-to-make whittled toys is shown in Fig. 1, at D, a penguin which waddles along in the most life-like manner imaginable. All the parts are cut from ½-inch white pine or other soft wood. The body and head are in one piece, but the beak is a separate piece, and the eyes are made of thumbtacks. Make the penguin about 12 or 15 inches tall. The wings and legs are cut from ¼-inch wood and pivoted to the body by small nails or screws driven through oversize holes. The legs will move more freely if a thin metal washer is placed over the screw or nail between each leg and the body. Drill a hole in the penguin's back for the ½-inch dowel rod which is used to push him along the floor, flipping his legs and wings like a real bird. When the penguin is completed, he should be painted black and white as indicated in the drawing.

The toy boxers shown at E will light into each other in earnest once they are properly rigged up and set in motion. Each is a jointed figure whittled out of ¼-inch soft wood. The heads and bodies are in one piece, but the arms and legs are separate and are fastened to the bodies by means of thin wires passed through holes and twisted over at the ends. Pass another piece of flexible wire through the hole where each boxer's arms join his body, and twist the ends of these two wires together so they form a circular loop as shown in the drawing. Then tie a piece of string to each side of the wire loop. Hold the strings, one in each hand, and draw them fairly taut. Then place the boxers on a table and jounce them up and down. Legs and arms will fly, and there will be a battle royal for as long a time as you care to keep it up.

The little trick stick shown at A, Fig. 2, is probably the easiest to make of all the things described in this book, but make no mistake, you can have a lot of fun with it. Cut the stick from a piece of ⅛-inch or thinner wood, and make it about 4 inches long and ½ inch wide. Round the ends and drill a hole near one end. Pass a piece of cord through the hole and knot it to form a loop just a little too short to pass over the lower end.

The trick is to loop the stick to a buttonhole in the lapel of a boy's or man's suit coat. You do this, unobserved. It is then up to the other person to try to get it off. To fasten the stick in a buttonhole, you must first spread out the loop till it forms a circle and then place it around the

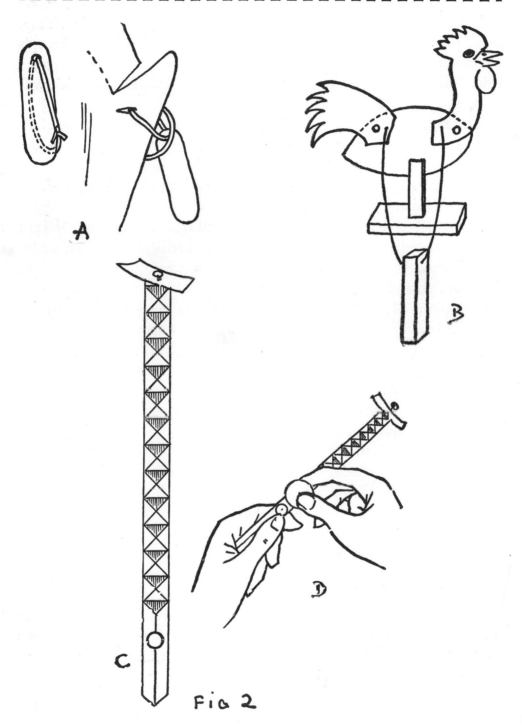

A

B

C

D

Fig 2

hole, so the hole is in the center of the circle formed by the string. Then draw the cloth through the loop until enough has been pulled through to permit the stick to be pushed through the buttonhole from the under side. Then push the cloth back into its original place and the stick will be securely looped into the buttonhole.

To remove the stick, the loop is placed around the hole and the cloth drawn up through it as before. The stick is then passed through the hole from the upper to the under side and will be free.

At B, Fig. 2, is a rooster whittled from ⅛-inch thick soft wood. It bobs its head and tail in a most lifelike manner when the wooden pendulum attached to these parts is swung to and fro. The various parts are fastened together by two bolts with nuts screwed over the ends or by nails bents over at the pointed end. These are passed through oversized holes so the head and tail will move freely. The base for the bird is made of two pieces of wood, a flat piece for the whole to rest on, and a square or round upright piece with a slot cut in the upper end to hold the rooster's body. When completed, place the rooster on the edge of a table or mantelpiece and start the pendulum swinging.

The notched magic stick shown at C is cut from a piece of wood about ½ inch square and 6 inches long. Along one of its edges cut a series of V-shaped notches, and to one end attach a little wooden propeller, fastening it to the stick by means of a pin. When the toy has been made, it is operated as follows. Hold the stick in your left hand and with the right hand rub a coin rapidly back and forth over the notches. In a few moments the vibrations set up in the stick will begin to take effect on the little propeller and will cause it to whirl around.

With a little practice you can control the propeller and change the direction of its spinning at will, by changing the positions of the first and second fingers of the right hand. In holding the coin between the thumb and first finger of the right hand, allow the end of the first finger to extend over the top of the stick and bring the second finger close beside it, as shown in the right-hand drawing at D. To make the propeller revolve from left to right, allow the end of the first finger to rub along the top edge of the notches. Then, to reverse the direction, relieve the pressure of this finger, and press the second finger against the other edge of the notches. At first you may not be able to make the propeller obey your commands, but with a little practice you will master the trick.

A thumbtack driven into the stick a little below the notches will add to the effectiveness of your show, when you exhibit the stick to your friends. Press your left thumb against the tack whenever you change the direction of the propeller. When you let a friend have the stick, he will invariably press or pull on the thumbtack, trying to find out how the motion of the propeller is controlled, but he will never discover the secret unless you tell it to him.

Another and final group of whittled articles is illustrated in Fig. 3. A wooden "snorer" or "buzzer" is shown at A. It is made from a piece of wood about 8 inches long, 2 inches wide, and ¼ inch thick. Cut notches in each of the four edges; then whittle one end down to a blunt point and bore a hole through the wood. Fasten a piece of cord about a yard long through the hole and swing the snorer around your head in a circle, when it will emit a queer, almost human sound.

Whittle the balancing doll shown at B from a piece of soft wood about 1 inch square. In each side of the body cut a slit for the insertion of the two balancing paddles. These are cut from ⅛-inch or thinner material and are fastened to the body by pressing them firmly into the slits, using a little glue if necessary.

It is important that the wings be of the same weight and be placed at equal angles to the body if the figure is to balance evenly on its pointed base; but it is very easy to make the wings match by cutting them from the same pattern, and if one is heavier than the other, to adjust its weight by whittling away a little at a time.

When completed, the figure should be painted in bright colors. Then, in addition to balancing on the cork of a bottle or even upon the eraser on the end of a pencil, it will spin around and bob from side to side and backwards and forwards as though it were really alive.

An old favorite—the monkey on a stick—is shown at C. His body and arms and legs are cut from ⅛-inch or thinner material, and are joined together by pieces of wire with the ends bent over or covered with glue to hold them in place. When the monkey has been made, get two pieces of wood, each ¼ inch square, one piece measuring 1 foot long and the other about 2 feet long. Drill a small hole through each stick near one end.

The Snorer — A

Balancing Doll — B

Monkey on a stick — C

The Gymnast — D

Dancing Sailor — E

Stern-Wheel Paddle Boat — F

Snap in Block — G

Fig. 3

Now fasten the monkey's feet to the shorter stick by passing a pin or a piece of wire through his feet and the hole in the stick, and bending the ends over to keep it from slipping out. In the same way fasten the monkey's paws to the longer stick. Then fasten the two sticks together by means of two strips of tin or copper. These are bent around the sticks and tacked to the longer stick only, so that the shorter stick can move freely up and down. The monkey is then made to perform his tumbling antics by moving the shorter stick up and down.

The gymnast shown at D, Fig. 3, is whittled out of ⅛-inch soft wood, and the arms and legs are fastened to the body by means of wires or pins. Build the stand of any light wood. It consists simply of a base and two uprights, through each of which is drilled a hole large enough to accommodate a knitting needle or a length of ⅜-inch dowel.

When the stand has been made, push the knitting needle or dowel through the hole in one of the uprights, through the hands of the gymnast, and then through the hole in the other upright. If the hands do not fit tightly, fasten them with glue. If a piece of dowel is used, it can be fitted with a handle made from a piece of bent wire. Now by turning the needle or dowel the gymnast can be made to go through his paces. To make him both more lifelike and more spectacular, he should be painted in bright colors.

Another jointed figure which is fun to make and fun to play with is the dancing sailor shown at E, Fig. 3. He is cut from ⅛-inch material and fastened together by means of pins or wires bent over at the ends. All the parts should be loosely jointed so they will move freely. A length of black thread is knotted around the sailor's head.

To make Jack dance the hornpipe, tie two small safety pins to the ends of the thread and fasten the pins in your trousers at the knee. Adjust the length of the thread so that when you sit on a chair, the thread will stretch in a straight line from knee to knee. Put a lively tune on the phonograph or turn on some dance music on the radio. Then keep time to the music by tapping your heels up and down. Every time one of your feet moves, Jack's arms and legs will swing about and he will dance in such a funny and lifelike way that the audience will be convulsed with laughter.

The stern-wheel paddle boat at F, is one of the simplest kinds of a self-propelled boat that can be built; but it is one of the most reliable and satisfactory boats, for it will always go and it will travel a considerable distance with one winding.

The hull is whittled out of a flat piece of wood measuring 12 inches long, 3 inches wide, and ½ inch thick. These measurements may be altered, of course, to suit your own preference. A rectangular opening 3 inches deep and 2 inches wide is cut in the stern. The paddle wheel consists of a single piece of wood 3 inches long and 1½ inches wide. A shallow groove should be cut from side to side across its center to hold the rubber band which furnishes the motive power, and notches should be cut in the two projecting struts for the same purpose.

To set the boat in motion, fit a thick rubber band over the struts, put the paddle wheel between the two parts of the band, and wind it up backward as tightly as possible. Hold the wheel with your hands to keep it from unwinding prematurely; put the boat in the water, and away it will go.

A toy with which you can have a good deal of fun is the snap-in block shown at G, Fig. 3. It consists of a block measuring 1 inch square and 2 inches long with a ¼-inch hole drilled part-way through from one end. Into the hole slides a pin with a tapered head. A small hole is drilled in the top of the block.

The owner of the block holds it in his left hand and holds the plug in his right hand. He inserts the end of the plug in the hole. Suddenly it snaps out of his fingers into the block. Some think that there is a rubber band hidden inside the block; others that a vacuum is created in the hole. When spectators are given the block to examine, they invariably spot the little hole, and think that it contains the secret. They will try to make the plug snap into the block by covering the hole with their fingers; but nothing will happen and they will have to give up.

Actually, the secret is simplicity itself. All you have to do is to hold the plug between your right thumb and forefinger, put its end in the hole, and then increase the pressure of your thumb and finger on the tapered end. At once, as you do this, the plug will be forced out of your grip and will snap into the block like greased lightning.

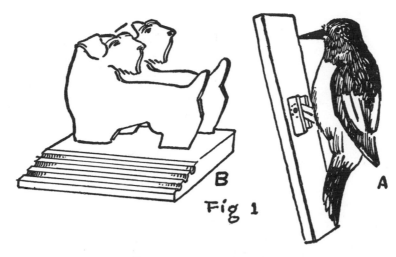

Fig 1

## USEFUL GIFTS

A WOODPECKER door-knocker is shown in Fig. 1 at A. The wood-pecker is a silhouette whittled out of ¼-inch wood. When completed, it is mounted on a nail between two small wooden uprights nailed to a wooden base. When the woodpecker's tail is lifted, its beak raps smartly against the wooden base.

A useful letter holder and pen rack, which makes an attractive Christmas or birthday present, is shown at B. The two dogs are whittled from ¼-inch soft wood and are fastened with thin nails and glue to a wooden base, in which are gouged out one or more grooves for pens or pencils. Other figures—such as bears, elephants, cats or rabbits—may of course, be used instead of dogs.

The duck shown at C is a quaint bird whose beak and topknot are formed by a pair of scissors. Her wings are pin-cushions and she keeps a wary eye on the spools which line her nest. She makes an amusing present for someone who likes to sew.

Draw the duck's outline on a piece of 1-inch soft pine, and whittle out its figure. Drill a hole through its head for the scissors and drill another hole in its back. A short piece of dowel or other circular wood is glued into the latter hole to hold the thimble. The wings are made of velvet or velour shaped over cotton, hair or moss, and glued to heavy cardboard backing pieces. The latter are glued to the duck's sides.

Whittle out a circular base for the spools and drill six holes in it to hold short pieces of dowel for the spools. Then fasten the circular piece to the base by means of glue and nails driven upward through the base. Finish the duck and the other parts with white enamel or with bright, gay colors.

The cocker spaniel and Scottie drawn in 1-inch squares at A, Fig. 2, are to be set on the lawn to carry the house number so that it can be plainly seen. Cut the dogs from 1-inch thick white pine and paint them in appropriate colors. The numbers are whittled from ¼-inch white pine and are painted white. They are fastened to the dog by means of brads. Drill a vertical hole in one front and one hind leg, and insert a piece of stout wire in each hole, securing it with glue or cement. Then drive the wires into the ground to hold the dog in place at the spot chosen for him.

The donkey and Mexican shown at B, Fig. 2, are intended for use as flower pot holders. Each is a whittled silhouette cut from white pine and decorated in gay reds, yellows and blues. They are fastened to the base pieces by means of brads driven upward through the bases. The Mexican's flower pot is placed on the base near one end. The donkey carries two small pots. These are inserted in panniers which are coasters for tumblers made of raffia or other material, such as can be purchased at most of the five-and-ten cent stores.

At C, Fig. 2, is shown a wooden butterfly, whittled from ½-inch soft wood and painted in bright colors. Its body consists of a glass test

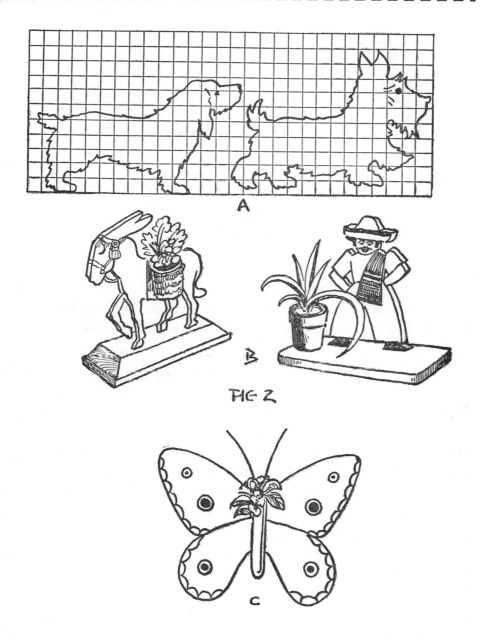

A

B

FIG 2

C

tube such as can be bought at any druggist's for five cents. **This is** fastened to the wooden wings by means of two wire loops that pass through small holes drilled in the wood. When completed, the butterfly forms a gay wall vase, the test tube being filled with water and flowers.

Fig 3

Another group of whittled novelties is illustrated in Fig. 3. The box shown at A is a string holder. A square wooden box may be purchased or found in the attic, or else you can make the box yourself from ¼-inch soft wood. The cover should be removable so the ball of string can be placed inside. Draw the outline of the bird on a piece of ½-inch wood and cut it out with your pocket knife. Then paint it in any gay colors you prefer. When the paint has dried put a small screw eye in the bird's mouth. The end of the string is passed through the screw eye which makes it easy to get hold of. Glue the bird to the top of the box and he will look as though tugging at a worm.

The dog shown in Fig. 3, at B appears to be holding a child's toothbrush in his mouth, although the brush is actually supported on the two small hooks screwed into each side of the dog's chin. Draw the outlines of the dog's head on a piece of ½-inch soft wood, and then whittle it out with your knife, and paint it brown or black and white. Screw the two small hooks in place to hold the brush, and put a screw eye in the top of the dog's head by which to hang it up on the bathroom wall. The toothbrush does not have to be laid horizontally across the hooks. Instead, two toothbrushes may be suspended vertically from the hooks.

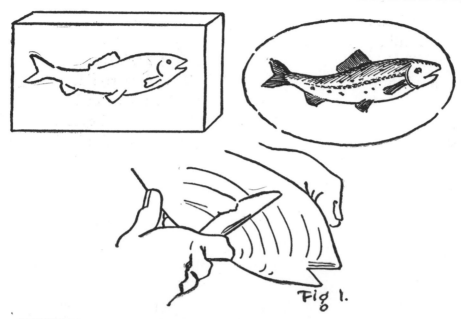

Fig 1.

## WHITTLED ANIMAL AND HUMAN FIGURES

WHITTLED animals and human figures are easier to make than one would suppose. Start with the simpler figures and work up to the more finished ones, and you will have no difficulty in acquiring the small amount of skill that is required. And, once you have learned to turn out Scotties, horses, elephants, and grizzled old sea-captains, you will have discovered one of the most fascinating of all whittling hobbies. Moreover, there is no reason why your hobby should not also be a source of profit, for small hand-carved figures have become popular and are sold in hundreds of stores in all parts of the country. Dozens of people are using their whittling skill to add to their income, and there is room for many more, for hand-carved figures are prized more highly than those that are machine-carved.

One of the easiest figures to carve is that of a fish, and carefully whittled, well-painted reproductions of real fish are exceptionally handsome. Mounted on wooden plaques, they can be sold or given away to friends who are ardent fishermen. To get colored pictures of fish to copy, get books on fish from your library or get the copies of the National Geographic Magazine at the library that contain color-plates of fish. There is also an excellent book containing color-plates that can be bought at many five-and-ten cent stores.

Fig. 1 shows a whittled model of a brook trout. The outlines are first drawn in pencil on a block of soft pine and the waste wood outside the lines is whittled or carved away. If the fish is to be mounted, you need finish only the front side. The reverse side is merely roughed out. Whittle the outline down to give the needed curves, and finish off with sandpaper. Outline the gills, mouth and eyes with shallow cuts to bring them into relief. The scales are outlined with a hard pencil, the rear edge of each scale being scored to make it stand out. Make the heavy back scales deeper than the light ones on the underside.

The fins are cut from thin pieces of pine and are glued or cemented in place.

Painting the model is the most absorbing part of the work, for it turns the plain wooden form into a brilliant, lifelike figure. Apply a priming coat of shellac, then a base coat of artists' chrome yellow oil paint. Then apply the other colors, blue, green, red or yellow, depending upon the fish. Blend the colors carefully, using your finger to soften the tints and shade one color into the other. Then paint in the eyes, mouth, and body markings. The scales will stand out as the paint dries, each edge highlighted as in a real fish.. Let the paint dry for several days and then coat the model with a clear 4-hour varnish, which will give it a lifelike sheen.

Mount the model on a white pine plaque either by means of two wooden pegs or by driving two nails through the back of the plaque into the fish's body.

Next try your hand at some life-size birds. When these are carefully rounded and painted in characteristic colors, it is amazing how closely they resemble real birds. See Fig. 2. They can be used for table or mantel decorations or for garden ornaments. Smaller models can be used to decorate flower pots or curtain pulls, or for other purposes.

Get a bird book from the library, book store or ten cent store, and trace the pattern of the bird of which you wish to make a model, on a piece of tissue or other thin paper. Then transfer the tracing by means of carbon paper to a block of soft pine or balsa wood of the required size.

It is usually best to make life-size bird models in three parts, one for the head and body, one for the bill, and one for the tail. When you

FIG 2

*hummingbird* *Goldfinch* *Baltimore Oriole* *Bluejay* *Cardinal* *Wire Leg* *4 wires* *Redwing Blackbird*

have traced the outlines of the head and body on the wood, rough them to shape with your knife, drill a hole for the bill, and saw or cut out a slot for the tail. When shaping up the body, cut grooves in the back to reproduce the wing tips and feathers. The tail should also be grooved to show the tail feathers. Your bird book will show you these details. Eyes for small birds can be made from black-headed costume pins, set in a small socket to keep them from bulging. For large birds, it is best to buy glass eyes from a taxidermist.

The legs will do a great deal to give your modeled birds a characteristic, lifelike appearance. Some birds, such as humming birds, swallows and flycatchers, usually perch with their legs drawn up under them. For this reason, the models of these birds need no legs. Other birds, however, like robins, woodpeckers, blue jays, grosbeaks and finches have characteristic legs that are always visible. Legs for these birds should be made of thin wire glued into holes drilled in the model. To show the four claws, twist four strands of wire together and separate them at the bottom to form the claws.

Whittled models of the ordinary birds may be mounted on small branches or placed on a bookcase or mantelpiece to serve as unusual decorations. Models of wild ducks and geese, smaller than life-size, but accurately colored, make very striking wall decorations when

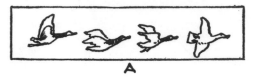

A

B

FIG 3

C

mounted on wooden panels painted to show a background scene of water and a bit of shore line, such as those shown in Fig. 3. It is best to whittle ducks and geese from a single piece of wood. After you have done some rounded silhouettes with upraised wings, such as those in the panel shown at A, try some with one wing spread horizontally or at an acute angle from the body, like the two shown at C.

Scottie dogs of the types shown in Fig. 4 are among the most popular of all whittled animal figures. They can be used in dozens of ways—as ornaments, as book ends, as decorations for box tops, and so on. You can make them as small or as large as you like.

To whittle a Scottie, draw his profile outline on a block of soft wood. The block may be ½ inch, ¾ inch or more in thickness. To start with, use a ¾-inch thick block, which makes a popular sized dog. It is best to have the grain run lengthwise or from head to tail. Care must be taken in shaping up the ears when the grain runs in this direction, to prevent them from breaking.

Cut away the block down to the outlines of the dog, using either a knife or a scroll saw. Then begin to round up the edges. Cut along the line of the jaw and take out a V to form the neck, then separate the ears and curve them in back.

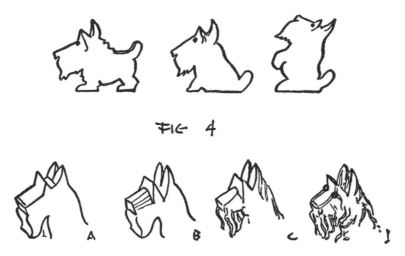

FIG 4

Next carve the face, following the successive drawings in Fig. 4. The space between the ears and the peaked forehead is cut out, and the nose is whittled to shape step by step as shown. Then small V-shaped pieces of wood, as shown in the drawing, are whittled out to create the whiskers.

Finish rounding up the dog's body, and then make additional V-cuts to give the appearance of a shaggy coat such as Scotties sport. The eyes can be represented by cutting pyramid-shaped notches or by using pins with round black heads cut down to ¼ inch long and driven into the wood. These can be obtained at any ten-cent store. When completed, the dog should be painted black or dark brown. A good coloring material is India ink.

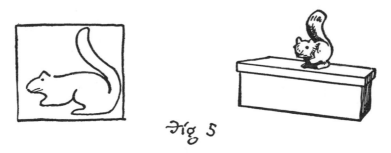

Fig 5

The squirrel shown decorating a box top in Fig. 5 is whittled out in exactly the same way as a Scottie dog. Other types of dogs, or models of your own dog, can be made without difficulty; and bears, horses, or even elephants, giraffes, hippopotami and rhinoceri can readily be fashioned out of wood by simply tracing their outlines on a block of soft wood of the required size and whittling them out. A deer or stag is a little more difficult because of their legs and the delicacy of the antlers; but many boys have created perfect replicas of these animals —just as the Swiss carvers do—and they well repay the patient work expended on them. A drawing of a deer model whittled by Arthur Dayton, a fifteen-year old boy of Bridgeport, Conn., is shown in Fig. 6. Also illustrated in Fig. 6 is a happy-go-lucky pig that is fun to carve and fun to look at.

FIG 6

Before going on to describe the whittling of human figures, attention should be called to the hobby of whittling matches to suggest animal and human shapes. (Fig. 7). A knife with a thin blade is needed and a reasonable amount of care and patience; but good results are far easier to obtain than you might believe at first glance.

How matchstick figures are made is illustrated in connection with a "Popular Science Monthly" contest. Legs and arms are curved by cutting, bending or breaking the wood as necessary, and applying a drop of glue or mucilage to the joint. Before splitting off the arms or separating the legs, it is best to dampen the wood. Single figures and groups can be preserved by pasting or gluing them to cardboard or wood and giving them a coating of shellac.

Step 1  Step 2  Step 3  Step 4  Making a deer

Dancing match figures  Boxers

FIG 7

Horseback Riding  The Prisoner

When you have whittled out a few Scotties or other animals, you will be ready to try your hand at a human figure such as the old down-East sea captain illustrated in Fig. 8. Other similar figures are displayed nowadays in many stores and can also be reproduced in wood by the amateur whittler. The drawings that show the steps followed in making the captain are adapted from illustrations that appeared in "Popular Science Monthly."

The captain is made from a piece of soft, straight-grained wood measuring 1½ inches by 2½ inches by 5½ inches. First draw ½-inch squares on the front and one side of the block as at A, Fig. 8. Then saw in along all the horizontal lines from the sides—the tops of shoulders, bottoms of coat sleeves, and bottom of coat. From the front and back, saw in under chin, at the back of the neck, at the front and back of the coat bottom, and the slot that separates trousers and shoes. This slot goes in ½ inch from the front of the block. Now saw the ⅛-inch wide slot between the legs.

The next step is to use your scroll saw, or knife if you prefer, to cut the blank to the shape shown at B, Fig. 8. Saw or cut away the waste wood at the sides of the head, and outside the arms down to the elbows. Cut up the outside of each leg to within ¼ inch of the bottom of the coat. Then saw or cut up the fronts of the trouser legs until you meet the saw cut that marks the bottom of the coat. Cut away the wood in back of the trousers, and then complete the cuts at the sides of the legs.

Next cut along the lines of the coat from elbows to bottoms of the sleeves, cutting downwards to prevent splitting the wood. Make the indentations at each side of the coat bottom, and then curve the front of the body as shown in the side view at A, using either a knife or a scroll saw. This completes the shaping up of the blank.

From this point on, the figure is whittled to its final lines, shown in Fig. 9. First draw the outlines of the sleeves on the front, back and sides of the blank and score the sleeve outlines with the point of your knife. Then, little by little, cut away the waste wood surrounding the sleeves until the block looks like the drawings at C, Fig. 8. The arms will then be roughly shaped and standing out from the body.

Next whittle the trousers and shoes to shape, following the drawings in Fig. 9, and at D, Fig. 8. Nick out the heels and round them at the back; then round the toe of each shoe and cut out a sliver of wood around each shoe to indicate the dividing line between uppers and soles. Then whittle off the corners of the trousers to give them the octagonal shape shown in D, Fig. 8.

Now start to work on the head. Measure down ½ inch from the top of the back of the head piece and draw a line across the wood at this point. Draw slanting lines on each side of the block, from the ends of the horizontal line to the top of the block at the front as at E, Fig. 8. Cut off the wood above the slanting lines. Draw an oval on top of the head piece, and whittle away the corners to round the piece as at F, Fig. 8. Then whittle the shoulders roughly to shape. Draw a line around the oval ½ inch down from the top to mark the joining of face and cap, and cut in this line about ⅛ inch deep. Then whittle away the wood below the line to give the block the shape shown at G, Fig. 8.

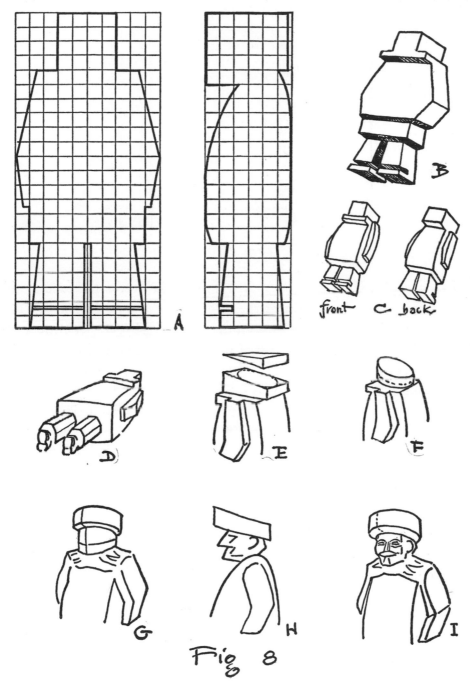

Fig 8

The face must now be whittled out, and the first step is to locate the nose. Draw a vertical line down the front of the block from the cap to the chin, as at G. Measure down ⅜ inch from the joining of the cap

FIG 9

and face, and make a cut ³/₁₆ inch deep straight across the face at this line. This line marks the tip of the nose. Now cut in diagonally from the point of the chin to the bottom of the ³/₁₆-inch cut. Whittle away the wood diagonally from the tip of the nose to the join of face and cap, and the face will appear as at H, Fig. 8.

Now mark a triangle for the nose, as at I, and cut the wood away at each side. Outline the cheek bones with lines ¹/₁₆ inch deep sloping downward from the nose, and cut a slit for the mouth (See Fig. 9.) The eyes are made by cutting out notches, and a little hole is dug at the middle for the eyeball.

The cap is whittled to shape next, following Fig. 9, and then the coat collar, lapels, collar and tie are outlined. Score quite deeply along these lines, and shave the wood away outside them so the parts will stand out. Go over the whole figure, bringing each part to its finished state, as shown in Fig. 9. Make the notches shown for sleeve creases at the elbows. Mark the button positions, drill small holes, and glue in ends of matches, cutting them off short.

This will complete the captain, except for painting. You may use whatever paints you have available—enamel oils are preferred. Make the coat dark blue or black with gilt buttons; and make the trousers white. The cap may match the coat or be painted white, and should have a gilt strap and emblem. The face is a flesh color, with a dash of deeper color at the nose tip, cheek bones and chin. Hair and eyebrows are white.

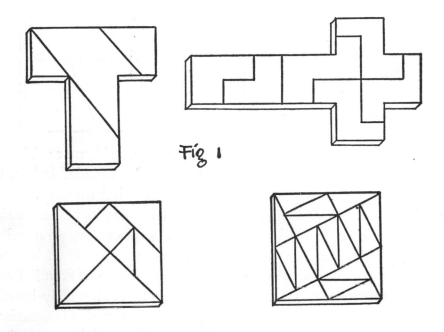

Fig 1

## PUZZLES

PUZZLES whittled out of wood are many and various. Some of them are simple to make and fairly easy to solve, while others, such as some of the dovetailed joint ones, belong in the class of "impossibles." No one can see how they could possibly be made without defying the laws of nature. Whittling puzzles and giving them away to your friends will keep you busy for hours on end. It is one of the grandest of all the hobbies.

We will start with a few easy-to-make puzzles, such as those shown in Fig. 1. It should be noted that, while all the puzzles described can be whittled with a good pocket knife, they can also be made by using a jigsaw. Three-ply veneer is good material to use for the flat puzzles, if they are made with a jigsaw. This material is a little too tough to cut easily with a knife.

To whittle the T puzzle shown in Fig. 1, draw its outline and the interior lines on a piece of ⅛-inch soft pine, and cut along the two slanting interior lines with the point of your knife. This will make four separate pieces that will be more difficult than you would imagine to fit together again into the form of a T.

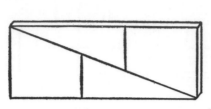

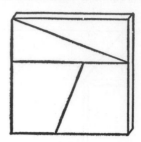

The Cross puzzle is made in the same way, but is a trifle more elaborate and difficult to solve, as are the two Cut-up Squares included in Fig. 1.

The Square and Rectangle puzzle is a mathematical mystery. If the square is cut with 8-inch sides, it will measure 64 square inches, according to all good arithmetic books. When the same pieces are arranged to form a rectangle, however, the latter will measure 5 by 13 inches, and contain 65 square inches. Where did the extra inch come from? Probably there is an answer, but it does not seem to be at all widely known.

Two "plug" puzzles are shown in Fig. 2. The first, which is sometimes called the "wedge-plug" puzzle, consists of a piece of ¼- or ½-inch soft pine in which are cut three holes—one a circle, one a triangle, and one a square. The old story is that a king once upon a time offered half his kingdom to anyone who could make a plug that would fit the three holes. Though many tried, all failed, until the court jester finally whittled out a plug of the shape shown. Such a plug is most easily made by starting with a piece of dowel. Cut off a piece that has a length equal to the diameter, and then taper curved sides to a fine edge, as shown.

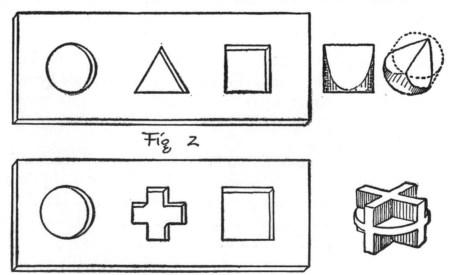

Fig 2

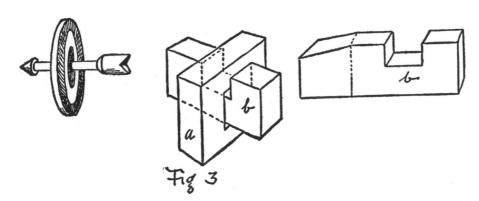

Fig 3

The "cross-plug" puzzle requires a plug that will fit three holes, one of which is round, one square, and one cross-shaped. The plug that solves the puzzle is cut from a piece of dowel or other cylindrical wood, and is shaped as shown in the drawing.

The two puzzles shown in Fig. 3 appear to be "impossibles" to those to whom they are shown. In each, a piece of wood is passed through an opening entirely too small to receive it. The secret of the puzzles is the fact that soft wood swells or becomes pliable when immersed in hot water or steamed.

In the arrow-and-target puzzle, make the target of white pine about 3 inches in diameter and ⅜ inch thick, with a ½-inch hole through the center. Then whittle out an arrow about 5 inches long, with both ends too large to pass through the hole. Soak the target for about two hours in warm water and the wood will swell. This will enlarge the center hole sufficiently to permit the arrow to be pushed slowly through it. Whittle down the point of the arrow a little bit, if necessary. When the wood dries, the target will shrink back to its original size and you will have a puzzle that will mystify your uninitiated friends completely. For Valentine's Day, you can make a wooden heart instead of a target.

In the Interlocked Bar puzzle, the piece marked A is whittled out of some fairly hard wood such as maple, while the piece marked B is cut from soft white pine. When the B piece has been made, it is softened either by steaming or by soaking in hot water. One end can then be compressed in a vise until it is small enough to go through the opening in A, or else can be simply pushed through the hole in A. It can then be gently forced back to its original shape by pressure on the sides. When the wood has dried, the sloping end is cut off along the dotted line.

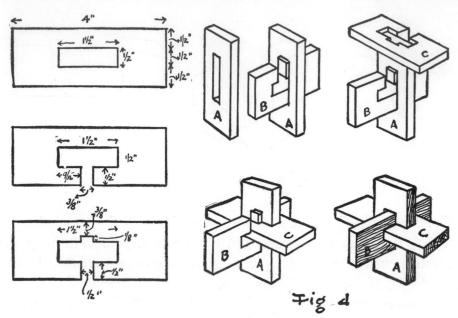

Fig 4

The triple Cross puzzle shown in Fig. 4 is one which you can ask your friends to try to put together. It consists of three pieces of ½-inch pine or other soft wood, whittled out to the shapes and dimensions shown.

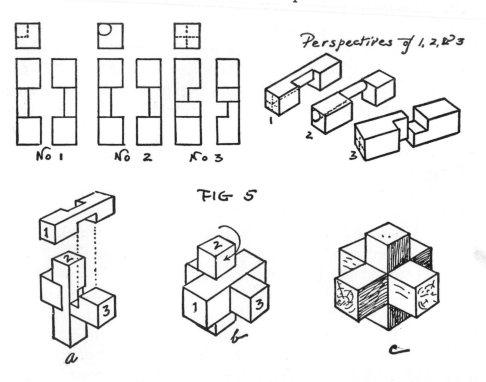

Perspectives of 1, 2, & 3

No 1    No 2    No 3

FIG 5

The steps in putting the pieces together and the finished appearance of the Triple Cross are shown in the subsequent drawings.

There are a number of so-called "burr" puzzles, ranging from the simple Three-Piece Burr shown in Fig. 5, up to the Nineteen-Piece Burr, which is sometimes called "The Great Pagoda." The three pieces of the Three-Piece Burr can easily be whittled out of soft white pine by following the drawings. If preferred, the pieces can be cut to shape with a fine-toothed saw. The first step in assembling the puzzle is shown at *a*. When all three pieces are fitted together, they will appear as *b*. Piece No. 2 is then given one-fourth turn to the right, which will complete the assemblage as shown at *c*.

The Six-Piece Burr is probably the most widely known of the burr puzzles. Machine-made specimens are on sale in many novelty stores under a variety of names. It is better fun to make your own, however, and to whittle as many as you like to give your friends. One piece, A, is a plain rectangular piece of wood, measuring 3 inches long and ¾ inch square. The other five pieces are of the same dimensions, but are notched in various ways. The method of assembling the puzzle is shown in the lower half of the drawing. (Fig. 6.)

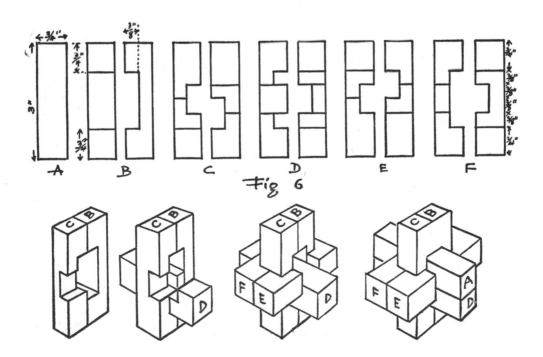

Fig 6

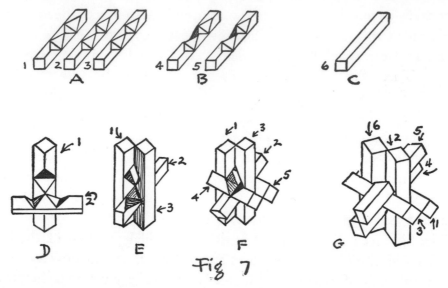

Fig 7

The Six-Piece Diagonal Burr shown in Fig. 7 is easy to make. This puzzle is also known as the Indian Six-Stick puzzle, since it was frequently made by the American redskins and probably originated with them. It has been used by Indians and others to form a knot on the head of a walking stick. This application is easy to carry out by squaring up the top of the walking stick to serve as the piece numbered 6, which is the key piece of the puzzle.

Use soft wood ½ inch square, and cut off six pieces, each 2 inches long. Piece No. 6 is left in its original square condition. Cut two notches in each of the five other pieces, as shown at A. Cut the notches carefully, making them right-angled so that one of the other pieces will fit in closely and evenly. Put three of these pieces—Nos. 1, 2 and 3—to one side. Then notch the two remaining pieces with a third notch, as shown at B. The pieces are now ready to be assembled.

Put Nos. 1 and 2 together at right angles, as at D. Then fit No. 3 against No. 1 and around No. 2, as at E, so that the upper notches of Nos. 1 and 3 form a square hole. Put pieces 4 and 5 horizontally each side of Nos. 1 and 3, with their center notches up as at F. The two notches in Nos. 4 and 5 will fit against pieces 1 and 3, partially surrounding these two latter pieces. Now push piece No. 6 through the square hole that is left in the center of the puzzle, parallel to piece No. 2, and the puzzle is assembled, as at G. If you wish, the ends of the pieces can

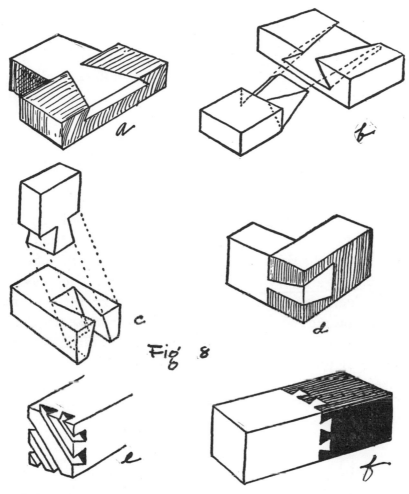

Fig. 8

be rounded with a knife, so that the assembled burr will be spherical. Different colors of wood may be used to give the puzzle added interest. And, as mentioned before, the burr may easily be assembled to form the head of a cane or walking stick.

Three intriguing dovetail puzzles are shown in Fig. 8. The T or Double Dovetail looks as though the impossible had been accomplished. The tongue, to all appearances, can not be moved either backward or upward out of the other piece, because it would have to pass through spaces that are entirely too small. How, then, was the tongue moved into its position?

The secret of the construction is shown at B. The dovetail is tapered and the tongue is inserted at an angle, not straight as would be naturally assumed. Whittle the two pieces out of ⅜-inch woods of contrasting colors. Make each piece about 2 inches long. Do the work carefully so the joint will be tight. If you wish to keep the secret from being discovered, glue the two pieces together and varnish the completed puzzle.

The two pieces forming the Right-Angle Dovetail are whittled out of woods of contrasting color to the shapes shown at C, Fig. 8. The light-colored piece is then slid down into position as at D. An opening will be left at the inside of the corner, and this must be filled with a triangular-shaped piece of the darker wood.

The dovetail joint that appears in the assembled Diagonal Dovetail puzzle is one that simply can not be constructed by ordinary methods. It is another sheer impossibility! This is because the dovetail ordinarily runs square with the sides of the block of wood. In the puzzle, however, the grooves are cut diagonally, as shown at E. Each block should be about 1 inch square and 2 inches long. Draw the lines marking where to cut on the end of one block and whittle it out; then make the other block to fit the cuts on the first. Use woods of contrasting color such as pine or poplar and mahogany. When the puzzle is completed the two blocks may be glued together and varnished to prevent the secret from being discovered.

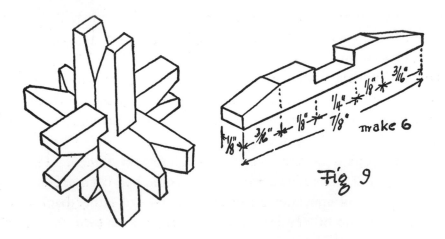

Fig 9

The Jackstraw puzzle shown in Fig. 9 is one that, theoretically, can-not be put together. However, by using small pieces about 1 inch long, and making the notches a trifle longer than required for a close

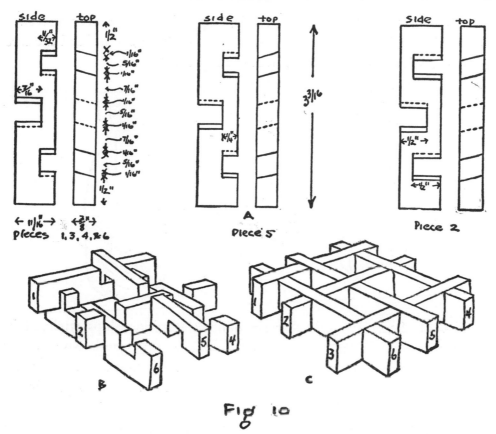

fit, the pieces can be forced into position. The individual jackstraws can be cut from square match sticks or from specially prepared wood about ⅛ inch square. The assembled puzzle has a novel appearance that will lead to many requests for "samples" and queries as to "how it is done." If the puzzle is to be handled very much, it should be strengthened by means of a drop or two of glue worked into the central joint.

The Grill puzzle shown in Fig. 10 is an extremely interesting one. It is fairly easy to make, but it requires care in assembling, and is as difficult to disassemble as to put together. To any but a woodworker or cabinet maker it appears to be an utterly impossible piece of work, because of the way in which the pieces weave in and out, overlapping each other.

The shapes of the six individual pieces are shown at A, and the method of assembly is shown at B. Pieces 2, 4, 5 and 6 are first arranged as shown at B. Then piece No. 1 is slipped into place over one end. When No. 1 is in place, the No. 5 piece is tipped back toward the left and No. 3 is slipped into place over the right-hand end.

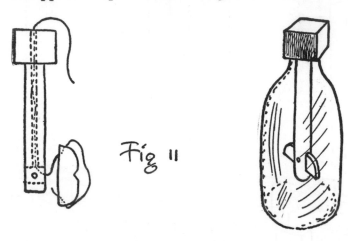

Fig. 11 shows a puzzle that resembles the sailing ships enclosed in bottles with necks far too small for the set-up masts and spars to pass through. In Fig. 11 a wooden rod with mortised-and-tenoned cross piece is seen inside a bottle, which has a mouth too small to permit the passage of the cross piece.

The wooden rod is made from a piece of dowel or is whittled from a straight piece of wood. The diameter is chosen to fit the neck of the bottle that is to be used; and a square wooden knob is glued to the top. When the glue is dry, whittle out the opening for the cross piece close to the bottom end. Then drill the vertical hole through the center of the rod that is indicated by the dotted lines.

Whittle out the cross piece, shaping it so it will fit closely in the opening made for it without being forced in. Then whittle out two little wooden pins to fit in holes drilled on each side of the rod opposite the cross piece. When the puzzle is assembled, it will appear that a single wooden pin passes right through the cross piece, holding it in place; but this is not the truth of the matter at all. The piece is a fake, made in two sections.

To assemble the puzzle, pass a piece of thread down through the vertical hole in the rod and out one end of the opening near the bottom. Make a small slit with your knife in each end of the cross piece, and put the thread in these slits, as shown. Now practice pulling the cross piece into the opening, before putting the rod into the bottle. Pull the cross piece half way in and then put a hat pin down the center hole and into the cross piece to hold it in place. Pull out the thread, and then work the cross piece all the way through by using the hat pin.

Now whittle out a thin cylindrical piece of wood to fill up the central vertical hole. Point the bottom end to fit into the notch in the cross piece. Put a little glue on the cylindrical piece and insert it in the hole. The top of the small rod can be hidden by gluing a thin piece of wood over the top of the square knob.

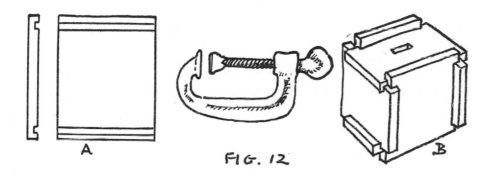

FIG. 12

The Chinese Savings Bank shown in Fig. 12 is not difficult to make and is one of the most interesting of the whittled puzzles. There are six pieces, all alike, except that a coin slot is cut in one piece. The shape and dimensions of the pieces are shown at A, and the assembled bank is shown at B. The bank is none too easy to put together, and three small clamps of the type shown in the drawing, and a block of wood 2 inches wide and about 6 inches long will be very helpful.

First fit the four side pieces around the slotted piece. Hold these in place with clamps, and force the bottom piece into place by forcing the clamped pieces outward with the 2-inch block of wood. When the bank has been assembled, the pieces may be a little bit loose, but they can be tightened up by soaking the bank in linseed oil. Once the bank is put together, it will be impossible to take it apart without breaking one of the pieces.

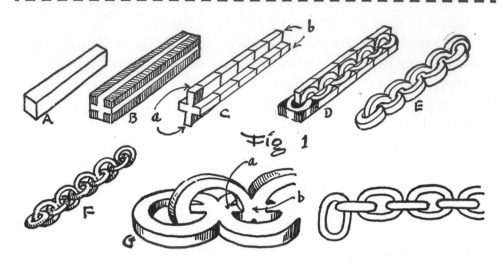

Fig. 1

## WHITTLED CHAINS
## AND INTERLOCKED RINGS

WHITTLED wooden chains and interlocked rings are among the most fascinating objects that can be made with a pocket knife. Once you have carved out a few of these seemingly impossible articles, you can class yourself as a true whittler in the great tradition of the art.

For careful work of this kind, it is best to use a penknife with a small thin blade.

Start by making a straight length of chain with oval links such as the one shown in Fig. 1. A well-made chain of this kind is ample evidence of your prowess as a whittler; and if you want to give it to some one to wear as a necklace or bracelet, the two ends can be fastened together with string or ribbon. Later on, you can tackle endless chains and chains with specially-shaped links.

Get a piece of straight-grained dry white pine or basswood measuring about 1½ inches square and 11 inches long, as at A. Divide each side into three ½-inch wide strips with a pencil, drawing lines along each side and across the ends, as at B. The next step is to cut away the four shaded areas. First whittle away the four edges. Then make vertical and horizontal cuts in to the border lines of the cross in the center of the wood, and carve away the waste wood. This part of the work can be simplified by sawing out the shaded parts with a coping saw or other fine-toothed saw.

Now you will have a long cross-shaped piece of wood, as shown at C. With a pencil, make marks at 2-inch intervals on the horizontal part of the cross, as shown at C. Then measure in 1 inch from the end, and mark off 2-inch intervals on the vertical piece. Darken with a pencil the 1-inch lengths at the end of the vertical piece, *a*, and the 1-inch lengths at the opposite end of the horizontal piece, *b*. Then whittle these short lengths off, and the wood will be in the shape shown at D.

The next step is to draw the semicircles that form the outside edges of the links. Then whittle V-shaped notches at each 2-inch mark. Round the notches up and the wood will appear as at E.

The next and last step is the most difficult. With a pencil, mark in the inside edges of the links as shown at the left of E. Then carefully whittle away each small semicircle inside each link.

When these have all been cut out, start to cut away the thin piece of wood that holds the first two links together. Work from the top, bottom and sides, making straight downward cuts, and then cutting toward these at an angle from the inside edge of the other link. Continue with the succeeding links, working slowly and bit by bit so as not to split or break the wood. At times you will find it convenient to use a sawing motion to separate the links. Go slow, and take it easy. That is the principle thing to remember.

As each link is cut free, round it up, and when you have reached the end, the chain will appear as shown at F.

One rule that should be carefully applied, particularly when whittling your first few chains, is to make each link good and long and to keep the links in the same plane, (that is, for example, all the vertical links) tight up against each other. If these precautions are followed, the work will go much more easily. What these rules mean in actual practice is shown at G, Fig. 1. Make the parts such as *a* as long as possible, and make *b* as short as possible.

When you have begun to get the knack of whittling chains and separating the links, by making one or more simple straight chains, you can try your hand at making a chain with one of the different link shapes shown in Fig. 2, rather than the oval links shown in Fig. 1. Circular links are easy, as are also diamond-shaped links. The figure 8 link is more difficult, but it is very effective in a finished chain. It is laid out

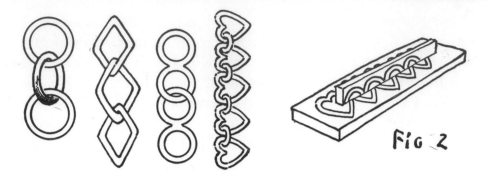

Fig 2

just as in Fig. 1, but each link is made double or in the shape of a figure 8. The hearts and circles require a cross-shaped block of wood with one pair of arms twice as broad as the other; that is, a block measuring, say, ¾ inch by 1½ inches. The method of laying out the links is indicated in the drawing.

There are several methods of making an endless chain, of which two are described here. Chains of this type may be made of pine or basswood, but many whittlers prefer a better wood such as maple, walnut or oak, for the finer finished effect.

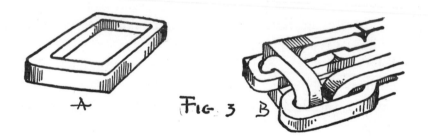

A          Fig 3          B

For the first method, whittle out a rectangular framework of wood, such as that shown at A in Fig. 3. Make this framework about two-thirds as long as you wish the finished chain to be. Then proceed as in Fig. 1, dividing each side of the framework into three strips of equal width, and cutting away the edges to form a cross. Next draw in the outlines of the links, making one link at each end as at B. The grain should run lengthwise of the framework, so that the two end links will be the only ones that will have to be cut across the grain, with the consequent risk of splitting the wood. The chain is then cut out in the same manner as the simple straight chain illustrated in Fig. 1.

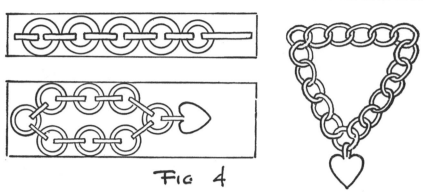

FIG 4

The second method of making an endless chain is illustrated in Fig. 4. For the chain shown, use a straight-grained block of wood measuring 10 inches long, 3¼ inches wide, and 1½ inches thick. Draw the outline of the chain on the top and each side, as shown, and then carefully whittle away the shaded parts of the wood. Each link has a diameter of 1½ inches and is ¼ inch thick, with the exception of the small link at the bottom attached to the heart. It is 1 inch or less in diameter.

Commence your whittling by carving away the shaded parts shown in the side view of the chain at A, except the shaded parts inside the links. When you have done this, you will have a block of wood ¼ inch thick with the semicircular outlines of the nine vertical links projecting above and below it.

You will now have whittled away the marked-in outlines of the eight horizontal links, which were used as a guide when first laying out the chain. Draw in their outlines on the ¼-inch block, making each 1½ inches in diameter. A pair of dividers will be a help to make the circles perfect.

Now work slowly, and cut away one link at a time. This will help to prevent the wood from breaking. Leave the heart until the last, for the end piece from which it is carved makes a handy piece to hold onto or to clamp in a vise while the links are being whittled out. When all the links have been cut loose, they can be rounded and smoothed with sandpaper. Instead of a heart as an ornament, you can carve a cross, an anchor, or any other device that suggests itself.

Probably the most unique whittled chains are those made from matchsticks. Various human and animal figures can also be whittled out of matchsticks, and these are described in another chapter. While match-

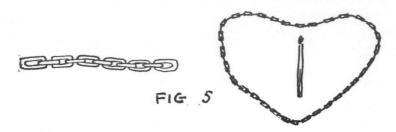

FIG 5

stick work seems almost impossible at first glance, just try it and you will discover that it is not really difficult and that it yields fascinating results.

Use the large wooden matches, sometimes called "kitchen" matches, and work with a small, very sharp knife blade. Lay out a straight matchstick chain just as in Fig. 1, cutting the matchstick down to the cross shape, and then separating each link. Use needles to eat away the wood between the links, unless you have a very finely-pointed knife blade.

To make a long chain, whittle out eight or ten matchsticks and then join the different chains together with silk thread. (Fig. 5.)

FIG 6

Closely allied to whittled chains are the interlocked rings, ovals and hearts shown in Fig. 6, all of which are favorites with experienced whittlers. The rings or other shapes that are to be whittled are first drawn with a pencil on a block of wood of the required size and shape, and are then carefully cut out with a sharp knife.

When whittling the triple rings, make the left-hand one tilt up from the center; and the two right-hand ones tilt down toward the center, and also down toward the top and bottom. This tilting is needed to make the rings flat, as they should be. The interlaced hearts are best

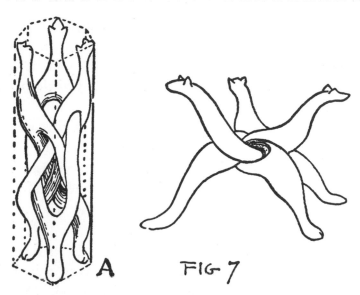

A    FIG 7

made by using the procedure shown in Fig. 1 for whittling a straight chain. Whittle a block of wood into the shape of a cross and then draw the two hearts as though they were the first two links in a chain. Point their pointed ends away from each other toward the ends of the block to provide plenty of room to work in when separating the links.

The interlocking tripod stand shown in Fig. 7 is an outgrowth of the interlocking ring idea. It is an old favorite with native carvers of the Orient and the West Indies, particularly Jamaica. Usually the interlocking pieces are given dog's heads, but occasionally they are made to represent snakes. The tripods are intended to hold incense burners, small bowls to serve as ash trays, or decorative crystal balls.

A fairly hard wood such as walnut, maple or mahogany should be used, because the nature of the design places the weight to be supported across the grain, and considerable strain is placed upon the ends of the links. It will simplify matters if you remember that the tripod is basically merely three oval links worked together just like three interlaced rings. The tripod looks more intricate than it really is. Actually, the design is regular and is easy to do for anyone who has whittled out the interlaced rings and similar projects.

Start with a block of wood measuring 1½ by 1¾ inches by 6 inches long, and shape this to a hexagon or six-sided piece as shown at A in **Fig. 7.** This drawing also shows the arrangement of the three pieces.

Begin your whittling by shaping up roughly the heads and necks of the dogs at the upper end of the block. Draw outlines of the figures on the wood and cut away the surrounding wood until you have the three parts separated, and roughly cut to shape. Then whittle out the dog's feet at the opposite end in the same manner.

After the heads and feet have been indicated in this way, begin to shape up the center section and cut in the lines of the dogs' bodies. Then work from one head toward the diagonally opposite foot, whittling out the two sides of the body. Go slowly and carefully, and the form of each dog will gradually emerge from the wood. Rough out one dog first; then proceed to the next one.

Soon each body will be whittled to approximately its final shape, and the three links will be formed. Then, using a very thin knife blade, separate the links by cutting away the interior wood. When this has been done, the tripod takes its finished form and will open outward. Smooth down the wood with your knife and then sandpaper it, and finish by waxing or shellacing.

One more article using the interlacing principle is the paper knife shown in Fig. 8. These make excellent and useful gifts. They should be whittled from a hard wood, such as walnut, pear or mahogany.

Select a block of wood ⅝ inch thick, about 8 inches long and 1½ inches wide. Draw the outlines of the knife as shown at A on a piece of paper or light cardboard, and cut it out with a knife and scissors. Place the pattern on one side of the block and run a pencil around its outline. Then do the same on the other side of the block. Now draw in the handle details, shown at A and B. These are different, for the parts interlace, and where one part crosses over on the top side, the other crosses under on the bottom.

The next step is to cut away the wood surrounding the knife and to cut out the interior spaces in the handle, indicated in the drawing by *a*. This will be made simpler if you drill small holes through each space to make room for the point of your knife blade to work in. These spaces can be cut out with a coping saw, if you prefer. Now work at each side, whittling down the wood until the ribbon-like parts of the handle are reduced to a uniform thickness. Shave down the ribbons at each intersection, to give the over and under effect, and then round off their

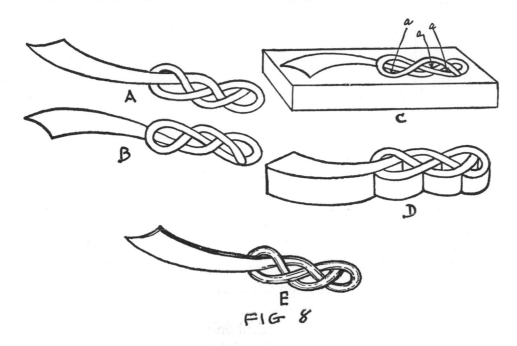

FIG 8

edges. The knife is then finished by beveling the edges of the blade and sandpapering all parts smooth. It can then be waxed and polished.

## CAGED BALLS AND RELATED FIGURES

A CAGED ball has long been one of the most interesting pieces of work that can be made by whittling. Essentially, the work is not difficult, but it does of course require a certain amount of patience and the necessary restraint to go slowly and carefully. It is almost inevitable that, when you show a caged ball to your friends, they will want to know "how it got inside"; and it is frequently difficult to convince them that both the ball and the cage have been whittled from a single piece of wood.

Start with a squared-up piece of pine measuring about 6 inches long and 1½ inches square. Mark the outlines of the cage bars by drawing straight pencil lines ¼ inch in from each edge and ¾ inch in from each end, as at A, Fig. 1.

Now draw two ¼-inch squares at diagonally opposite corners of one end of the block, as at x; and measure the distance between them, y.

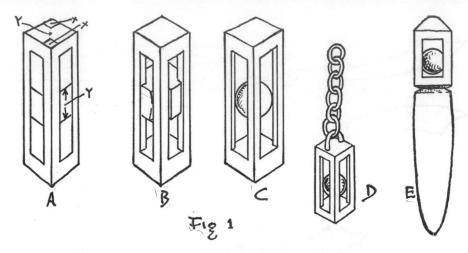

Fig 1

This gives you the greatest diameter of the ball that will turn in the cage. Lay out the distance y on the sides of the block, as indicated in Fig. 1, and draw the lines that mark its upper and lower ends, as shown in the drawing. These lines are marked on each side of the block, inside the cage bars. They indicate the size of the ball.

You are now ready to start whittling. Begin by drawing your knife blade along the lines marking the inside edges of the cage bars, making a fairly deep incision. Then draw your knife blade in the same way along the lines marking the top and bottom of the ball or central section. Continue by cutting out the waste wood at each end until the block appears as at B, Fig. 1.

The next step is to whittle out the ball from the square block of wood in the center of the cage. Begin by cutting small wedges off the corners of the block, slowly rounding them, and then gradually separating the block from the cage. When this has been accomplished, the center block will slide up and down. Continue taking small pieces off the block until it is a perfect round ball, but be careful not to make it so small that it will fall out of the cage.

When you have successfully completed your first ball-in-a-cage, you may wish to make smaller ones, cut from blocks ½ or ¾ inch square. These make good decorations to fasten with thread to a whittled chain. An effective chain and caged-ball combination is shown at D, Fig. 1, which is not difficult to make once you have got your hand in. A paper knife with a ball-in-a-cage handle is shown at E.

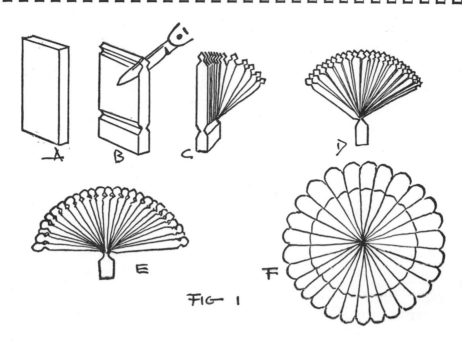

FIG. 1

## WHITTLED FAN FIGURES

WHITTLED fans are as popular and as dramatic an exhibition of the whittlers' art as the ball-in-a-cage figures. Like many other pieces of whittling work, fans look extremely difficult to make. Once the few simpler tricks of the craft are known, however, they are in reality very simple to whittle out. Then, by using the same method, some really extraordinary effects can be obtained, such as an Indian warrior in a feathered war bonnet or a peacock with a brilliantly-painted whittled fan tail.

The block of wood used for a fan should be of soft wood, such as pine or basswood, and should have a good straight grain. The width of the block may be anywhere from ¼ inch to ¾ inch. The thickness determines the width of the individual fan blades. For your first fan, use a block measuring ½ inch thick, 1 inch wide and 6 inches long, such as is shown at A, Fig. 1. Cut a notch in from both sides at a point about 1 inch up from the bottom of the block. Then shape the upper part of the block to the shape you wish the individual blades to be. At B, the blades are very simple—straight with straight-sided notches at the top. Other shapes are shown in subsequent drawings.

When the block has been notched, as at B, it must be softened by soaking it in water for from 12 to 24 hours, depending upon its thickness. The wood can also be softened in a shorter space of time by immersing it in boiling water for fifteen to twenty minutes.

When the wood has been softened, the blades of the fan are split apart as at B, care being taken that the knife blade does not cut below the center of the lower notch. Make each blade about ⅛₆ inch thick. Later, when you are familiar with the technique, you can make them as thin as ⅛₂ inch. Push the knife down through the wood slowly and make each split a straight one. Straight-grained wood will help in this, and is of real importance.

When all the blades have been cut apart, and while the wood is still throughly wet, the fan can be formed. Hold the base of the block in hand, and the tops of the blades in the other hand. Then twist the base one-quarter turn. This will begin the separation of the blades, and they can then be spread individually as at C. The tips of the blades can then be interlocked as at D, and the fan will be complete.

When the fan is finished, the base may be whittled to any desired shape to form a convenient handle.

The fan shown at E, Fig. 1, is made in the way just described, but has thinner and consequently more numerous blades. Also, the interlocking tips are rounded, instead of pointed. It is also possible to make circular fans, as at F, by using a wide enough block to provide the required number of blades. A block measuring ½ inch thick, 6 inches long, and 2½ to 3 inches thick will be needed for a circular fan. The handle is added after the blades have been completed.

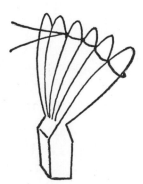

FIG. 2

Blades that are not notched at the upper end can not be locked together, but must be threaded. Two methods of threading are shown in Fig. 2. In the first, the center of a long piece of thread is placed against the edge of the right-hand or left-hand blade, and the ends of the thread are woven in and out over the blades, so that threads cross between each pair of blades. The second type of threading shown can be used when holes are made for the purpose near the tip of each blade.

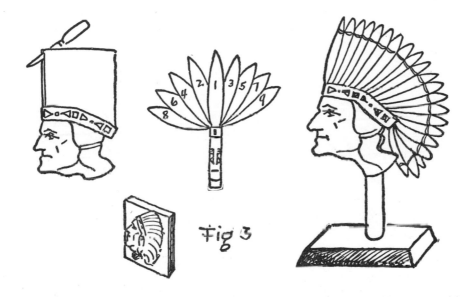

Fig 3

The Indian in his feathered war bonnet is shown in Fig. 3. Whittle it from a piece of soft wood ¼ inch thick, 2 inches wide, and 3 inches long. Make the notch to mark the base of the feathers just above the headband, and cut to it when splitting apart the feathers. When the feathers have been separated, they are spread out alternately. The first feather is left in place to be the foremost one of the head-dress. The second is bent to the left, the third to the right, and so on. When all the feathers are in place, they are threaded together. The Indian's head may be mounted on a vertical wooden bar or fastened to a base block or may be glued to a wooden panel.

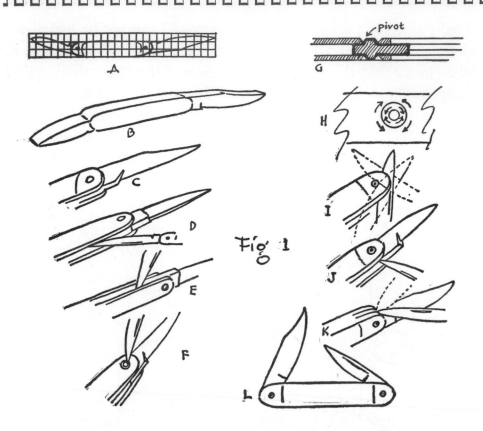

Fig. 1

## JOINTED FIGURES

WHITTLED figures with movable joints, such as knives, scissors, razors and pliers, represent another variation of the never-ending art of whittling. Figures of this kind are made from single pieces of wood and are, perhaps, the most difficult to execute. They demand skill and a very large degree of patience; but the rewards are well worth the effort expended. In addition to patience, you will need straight-grained soft wood, such as white pine or basswood, and a knife with a sharp, thin blade.

A wooden pocket knife with blades that open and shut on pivot joints is shown in Fig. 1. It is made with the blades in the open position, and they are closed after the knife is finished.

Draw the outlines of the knife, as shown at A, on a piece of 3/16-inch, straight-grained white pine or basswood, measuring 3/4 inch wide and 6½ inches long. The ¼-inch squares shown in the drawing at A can be laid out on your own piece of wood and will help in drawing the outlines of the knife. Whittle away the excess wood until you have the shape shown at B. Then thin down the blades until the ends are as shown at C.

Now cut out the inside of the handle. First cut around the inner edges of the handle, as at D, and then split out small wedges of wood. When you get deep inside the handle, you will have to cut diagonally at the base or butt of each wooden blade to shape it up as shown at E. Make a series of crisscross or X cuts at the bottom of the hollowed-out part to help in working the wood down to a level $\frac{1}{16}$ inch from the back. As you work, guage the depth of the hollow with the tip of your knife blade, to make sure that you do not cut through the back of the handle.

The next step—rounding the blade pivots and freeing the blades—is the one that requires the greatest care. Begin as at F, by cutting around the pivot with the tip of your knife blade, cutting out a V-shaped ring all around the pivot as shown at G. There is to be a circular pivot on each side of the wooden blade, each pivot revolving in a close-fitting circular hole. Work very carefully, and always cut with the grain as indicated by the arrows in H, to avoid splitting the wood. Cut the V-shaped ring down to a depth of slightly over $\frac{1}{16}$ inch (the thickness of one side of the handle). Cut a similar V-shaped ring round the pivot on the opposite side, making sure that the two sides of the pivot are exactly in line.

Now start to cut the butt of the wooden blade free from the surrounding wood. This is done by resting your knife blade on the side of the wooden blade and slowly working it in toward the pivot. When the first incision has been made to serve as a guide, work from all sides of the pivot, rocking your knife blade carefully to and fro, as indicated by the dotted lines in I. A razor blade should be used for this work if your knife blade is not thin enough. Cut in to the pivot itself, working your knife blade in until you can see its edge at the base of the V-shaped ring around the pivot at all points. The cutting from the inside of the handle is done as shown at J. When this work is completed, the wooden blade and pivot will be free at all points except at the joint at the back.

Cut two lines along the back of the handle, as at K, to indicate the metallic spring that butts against the heel of the blade of a real knife. Then work the tip of your knife blade into the back of handle at the point where the wooden blade meets the handle, rocking the blade a little, until the tip of the blade works through into the inside of the handle. Rounding out the heel of the blade, as at L, helps to get this part of the work done more easily. It is also a wise precaution to soak the wood thoroughly in water before doing this last bit of cutting.

It is now time to see if the blade will close. Try it very gently to see if it is free from the surrounding wood. If not, use your knife or razor blade to cut away the small bits of wood that still hold it. With a few final touches, the blade will soon close, and your wooden knife will be a success.

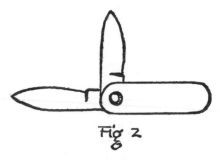

Fig 2

It is possible to make a knife having two blades on one pivot, such as the one shown in Fig. 2. Such a joint is just the same in principle as the one supporting a single blade, but the pivot must be made long enough to go through both blades. Niche the blade blank about ⅜ inch thick and do not shape the blades until you have whittled out and freed the pivot.

Other whittled figures incorporating pivot joints are shown in Fig. 2 —a razor, a pair of pliers, a padlock, and a little wooden door. The pivot in each of these figures is cut out in the same manner as that used in making the wooden knife.

Another joint—called the hinge joint—is used by whittlers, chiefly for whittling wooden pliers and scissors. How a pair of pliers is made is shown in Fig. 3.

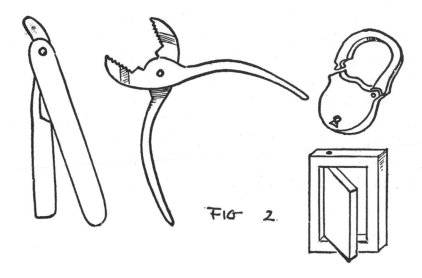

FIG 2.

Draw the outline of the pliers shown at A on a piece of soft wood ¼ inch thick, 1 inch wide, and 3¾ inches long. A larger piece—twice the dimensions given, for example, can be used if desired. Simply make ½-inch instead of ¼-inch squares to guide you in drawing the pattern.

Whittle out the blank for the pliers, B, and separate the jaws along the line a-b. Then cut wedges at points c and d, as indicated in drawing C. Both wedges are in the piece X and slant downward toward the piece Y. Turn the blank over and cut two more similar wedges in the opposite side of piece X. The wedges prepare the way for the next step, which is to make the piece X pass through a slot in piece Y.

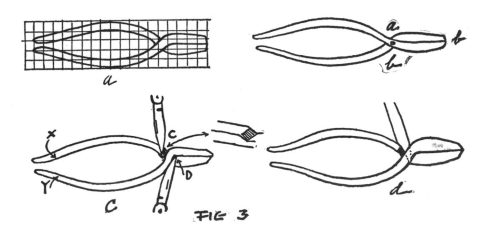

FIG 3

Now proceed to whittle out the slot by carefully pushing the tip of your knife blade into piece Y and rocking it back and forth to chew out the wood, as in D. Continue this process, working from both sides of piece Y and on both the top and bottom, until your knife blade has worked through piece Y and the two parts are separated. To be on the safe side, the wood can be soaked for an hour or so before doing the cutting-through. This will minimize the risk of splitting.

The pliers should now open. If they stick, open out the slot a little further by chipping away with the tip of your knife blade.

# WOOD CARVING

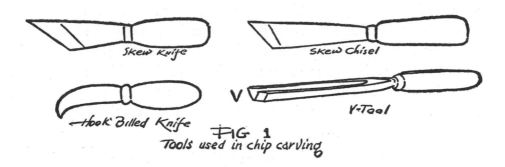

Skew Knife

Skew Chisel

V

V-Tool

Hook Billed Knife

FIG 1
Tools used in chip carving

## TOOLS AND WOODS USED IN WOOD CARVING

ANYONE who is taking up wood carving for the first time can start in with a very small assortment of tools. Then, as one's interest and skill increase, other tools can easily be added.

It has been said that the most necessary equipment for the beginner in wood carving is the urge to carve. This is the truth, for if one has seen carved work done by friends or accomplished craftsmen and feels the keen inner desire to duplicate it, a few tools and a certain amount of practice will soon develop the ability to carve.

## TOOLS USED IN CHIP CARVING

FOR chip carving work, which is one of the easiest and most popular forms of wood carving, the two most important tools are the skew knife and skew chisel. These are shown in Fig. 1, together with a hook-billed knife and a V-tool, which are also sometimes used in chip carving.

The skew knife has a thin blade and a long bevel on both sides of the cutting edge. As the illustration shows, the cutting edge is skew, or ground diagonally. When in use, it may be held with either one or both hands.

The skew chisel has a narrower blade than the knife and is usually the better tool to employ when making cuts in which the heel of the cutting blade is used. When making "toe cuts" with the toe of the blade, the knife is more efficient. The most commonly used skew chisel is one with a ¼ inch wide blade. Both tools can be purchased at any store dealing in carving tools, among which are hardware, handicraft and department stores. There are also several companies which specialize in furnishing tools and woods for wood carvers, and beginners would be well advised to write for their catalogues. Two of the largest companies of this kind are:—

Craftsman Wood Service Co., 2727 South Mary St., Chicago, Ill.

Albert Constantine and Son, Inc., 797 East 135 St., New York, N. Y.

Many craftsmen use the skew knife and skew chisel for all the cutting done in chip carving, but others prefer to use a hook-billed knife for making curved cuts. The V-tool is chiefly used to emphasize border lines or to separate different parts of a design. The use of these tools is explained in greater detail in the chapter on "Chip Carving."

The most important tools used by the wood carver are straight chisels, gouges, and V-tools. The latter are sometimes called parting tools. (See Fig. 2.) Sets containing six assorted tools—all that beginners will need—can be purchased for about three to four dollars. More elaborate sets containing nine or ten tools usually cost seven or eight dollars. The small sets, however, are entirely adequate for the beginner. One should not be too concerned about tools. Start in with two or three, and add others as you find you need or want them.

Straight chisels have a straight cutting edge, as distinguished from the diagonal edge of the skew chisel. The chisels used for wood carving, commonly known as "carving chisels," are ground with the bevel on both sides, instead of on only one side as in the case of the carpenter's and cabinet maker's chisel. Carving chisels are made both with straight and bent or carved blades. The beginner's kit may consist of straight tools; the curved types can be added later on, if desired.

Chisels are furnished with blades of various widths. Popular widths for beginners are ⅜ inch and 5⁄16 inch. These are the widths usually provided in the small six-tool sets with which most wood carvers start out. The ¼ inch, 5⁄16 inch, 7⁄16 inch, and ½ inch widths are also extensively used.

Chisels are used for cutting straight lines, for carving flat planes, and for blocking out convex round designs. Because of their straight cutting edges, they are not suitable for gouging out curved patterns or parts of a design.

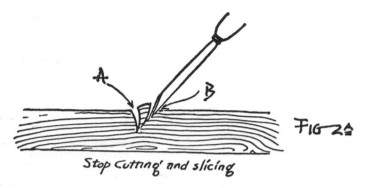

*Stop Cutting and slicing*

FIG 2ª

## STOP-CUTTING AND SLICING

FREQUENTLY, a chisel first makes a "stop-cut" to sever the grain of the wood and then cuts out a clean chip or "slice." This is done, for example, when modeling interlacing ribbon designs, as described under "Level Surface Carving." In Fig. 2a, the stop-cut is shown at A, and the second chisel stroke, or slice, is shown at B.

Gouges vary according to width and the curve of the cutting edge. (See Fig. 2.) These curves, which range from the almost imperceptible curve of the "extra flats" to the V-shaped curves of the veining and fluting tools, are known as the "sweep" of the gouge. The sweeps are known as the *quick*, the *medium*, and the *flat*, (Fig. 2), with a number of intermediate shapes to makes varied contours in carving. These tools may be purchased in various widths, ranging usually from ⅟₁₆ inch to 1 inch.

The small tool kits for beginners usually contains a ⁹⁄₃₂-inch gouge, which is actually a veining tool, (for veining leaves, outlining and grooving), and a ⅜-inch V-shaped gouge or fluting tool, the latter frequently having a bent or curved blade. The next size larger sets generally contain ¼-inch, ⅜-inch, ⁷⁄₁₆-inch and ½-inch gouges.

Gouges also vary according to the shape of the shank as shown in Fig. 2. There are four kinds, the straight shank, the long bend, the

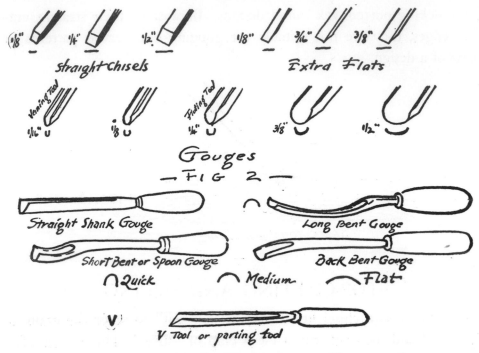

Gouges
— FIG 2 —

V Tool or parting tool

short bend, and the back bend. The beginner will not need any gouges having curved shanks.

Gouges are used for cutting out hollow curved forms and for finishing rounded surfaces and details. The gouge used should be the one of which the "sweep" most closely corresponds to the curvature of the surface or line to be cut. The veining tool is used for making thin shallow grooves and for finishing deep grooves.

A V-tool, or parting tool, is shown in Fig. 2. The most commonly used size is on with a ¼-inch blade. The parting tool is used for finishing inside corners, for outlining, and for undercutting. Because it is difficult to sharpen, roughing for V-grooving is generally done with a veiner.

To summarize the recommendations for the beginners tool set, a good six-tool set costing about $3.00 or less would contain:—

1 ⁵⁄₁₆-inch straight chisel
1 ⅜-inch bent chisel
1 ⅜-inch flat gouge
1 ¼-inch skew bevel chisel
1 ³⁄₃₂-inch gouge, or veining tool

Such an assortment will provide for the greatest scope of work possible with the number of tools involved.

All the above tools are furnished with both round turned handles and long octagonal handles. Some prefer the octagonal handles, claiming that they are easier to control, but the turned handles are apparently equally popular. Most experienced wood carvers like to have a variety of handles because they learn to associate the various tools with their handles and this enables them to pick out the tool they want more quickly from the selection lying on their table. This is a good plan for the beginner to adopt.

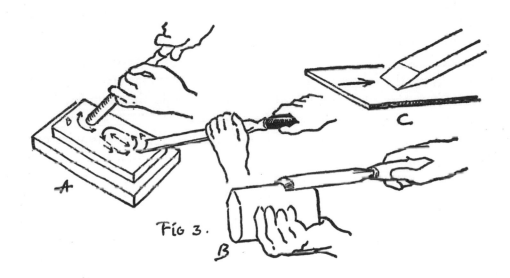

Fig 3.

## SHARPENING AND CARING FOR CARVING TOOLS

CARVING tools must be kept practically razor sharp, and it is essential that the sharpening operation be done with a good deal of care. Once a new tool has been well sharpened, it is easy to keep it in good condition by a little honing and stropping whenever it begins to be dull.

The equipment needed for sharpening the various chisels and gouges consists of an oilstone, several slip stones and a piece of leather dressed with fine emery paste. These can be purchased at the store at which you get your tools.

There are several types of oilstones, the most commonly used being the soft Arkansas and the Washita oilstones. The Arkansas stone is a hard natural stone and is a favorite with many wood carvers. The Washita stone is softer and sharpens the cutting edge more slowly, but gives excellent results. There are also stones made of carborundum and other manufactured materials.

When sharpening or honing a tool, a light oil mixed with a little kerosene should be put on the oilstone. This makes it cut faster. Fig. 3, at A, shows how a gouge is honed. First it is rubbed over the stone forward and backward, at at *a*. At the same time the gouge may be rolled from side to side. When it has been sufficiently honed in this manner, the gouge is rubbed over the stone as at *b*.

Slip stones are small, wedge-shaped stones, having either sharp or rounded edges. They are used for removing the burrs and wire edges from the inner sides of the U and V-shaped tools after they have been sharpened on the oilstone. The sharp-edged slip stones are used for removing the wire edge from V-shaped tools, while the rounded stones are used to remove the wire edge from gouges.

Fig. 3, at B, shows how a slip stone is used to remove the wire edge from a V-tool. Gouges are handled in the same manner, but a stone with a rounded edge is employed.

The final operation in sharpening a tool is shown in Fig. 3, at C. Here a chisel is being stropped on a piece of leather dressed with fine emery paste. As indicated by the arrow, the stropping is done in one direction only.

When you have finished using your tools for the day, the edges should be cleaned and oiled before they are put away. Experienced craftsmen sharpen and care for the edges of their carving tools as though they were expensive razors. Be careful never to drop a tool on the floor, and keep them either in the box in which they came or else in a roll of soft thick cloth fitted with pockets and a flap to fold down over the handles.

## OTHER EQUIPMENT

THE only other equipment needed for wood carving consists of a wooden mallet, some clamps of the type shown in Fig. 4, and a work

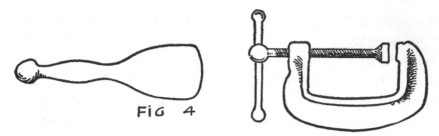

FIG 4

bench or table. If a cylindrical mallet cannot be obtained or you do not wish to buy one, a ten-cent store potato masher will be perfectly suitable instead. This type of mallet is used for wood carving, rather than the hammer type, because it will always hit the tool handle squarely and is of a more convenient shape for the striking of carving tools.

Clamps for holding pieces of carving wood firmly in place can be obtained at any ten-cent store or hardware store.

For a work bench, a kitchen table or other strong table may be used. If, after doing some experimental carving, you believe you have found a craft that will be a long-range hobby, you can get a regular carpenter's or woodworker's bench.

## WOODS FOR CARVING

It is best for beginners at wood carving to make their first experiments with one of the common and inexpensive soft woods, such as white pine or basswood. Experience has shown that beginners learn more rapidly and acquire a better technique when they carve the soft woods. The carving goes with less effort and the whole work is done more easily. Furthermore, the soft woods are the least expensive.

Basswood is obtained from the linden tree and is soft and easy to carve with sharp tools. It has a light tan or brownish tint, is fairly durable, and is not brittle.

White pine is similar to basswood but slightly harder. It contains more resin and has pink and yellow tints. When ordering at a lumber yard, ask for western, Pondosa, or select western white pine, as this is a less resinous and better carving wood than the fast-growing southern pine. Much of the early American architectural wood carving was executed in white pine, which at that time came from the eastern forests.

Butternut, yellow poplar, cottonwood and cypress are other woods that are easy to carve; and whitewood, sometimes called Tulip wood, obtained from a species of poplar, is another good wood for the beginner. It is comparatively inexpensive and takes a good finish.

California redwood is soft and has a beautiful red color; and sweet gum wood, also known as satinwood, is fairly soft and has a smooth and uniform texture which makes it excellent for carving. It is more durable than the woods previously mentioned and is suitable for furniture or other articles that may be subjected to wear or exposure. Its brownish color becomes deeper when the wood is varnished.

Slightly harder woods that are good for shallow cutting include sycamore, holly and beech.

Red cedar is not often used for carving, but is particularly good for chip carving as it cuts very cleanly. It is more or less knotty and can only be obtained in narrow pieces, so for carving is suitable only for small articles.

Among the hard woods used for carving, red oak, black oak and rock oak, are widely used. They are readily carved, yet are sufficiently hard to withstand wear and hard usage. For this reason they are used for chairs, tables, chests, and other furniture, as well as wooden boxes. American white oak is not recommended for carving, because it is very hard and presents many difficulties in carving.

American black walnut is another excellent hard wood for carving, as is also mahogany. Both have a close, even grain, but are easy to work. Cherry wood is quite extensively used for carving, as it takes sharp, clear cuts and wears well. It is hard to carve, however, and is usually obtainable in small pieces. It is frequently used to imitate mahogany, and when well stained and finished can be distinguished from mahogany only by an expert. Maple is hard, close-grained, and takes a good finish. It is suitable for carving medium-scale designs, standing between oak and mahogany in this respect. The bird's-eye, curly, and other figured species of maple are not usually carved, but are used as veneers because of the beauty of the grain.

When ordering wood from a lumber yard, carpenter or supply house, you should specify that it is to be planed, face and back, to the thickness desired. You should make plenty of allowance, however, in the length and width of the wood. When placing the design to be carved on a piece of wood, it is helpful to have an inch or so to spare around the edges, a surplus that is easily removed when finishing up the piece.

Be sure to specify that you want wood that has not been sandpapered. Sandpaper leaves particles of silica dust on the wood, and these will rapidly take the edge off a carving tool.

## CHIP CARVING

CHIP carving is one of the easiest kinds of wood carving and therefore one of the best for the beginner. The effects that can be produced are varied and extremely decorative and only a few tools are needed to carve out the most fascinating designs. As already mentioned, the tools used for chip carving are the skew knife, skew chisel, and hook-billed knife. As a matter of fact, practically all chip carving designs can be cut with the skew knife. Other tools that will be found convenient from time to time for this work include a parting tool $\frac{1}{32}$ inch to $\frac{1}{16}$ inch wide and a veining tool. In addition to these tools, you should have sharpening stones, clamps, and a mallet, all of which have already been described.

Chip carving was originated many hundreds of years ago by natives of the South Pacific islands, who used it to decorate paddles, adz handles, and other objects. Their cutting tools were sharpened shells or sharks' teeth. Chip carving was also widely practiced in Norway, Sweden, and other countries, largely for the decoration of household implements and furniture. It is frequently called "Frisian" or "Friesland" carving after a region in Germany where it was very popular and extensively used.

Designs for chip carving are made up principally of triangles, with either straight or curved sides, which are arranged in groups to produce interesting and ingenious patterns. Much of the effectiveness of the design depends upon the cleanness of the cuts and the sharpness of the edges, and for this reason woods are used that are soft and straight-grained. Red gum, yellow poplar, black walnut, mahogany and cypress are favorites with experienced chip carvers. Maple and birch are also

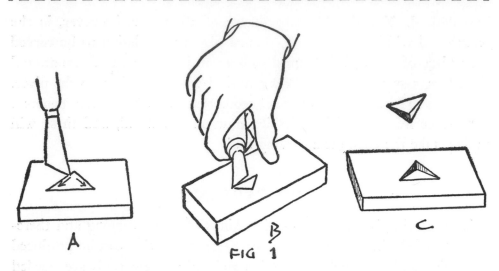

FIG 1

used, but they are harder and therefore more difficult for the beginner. Pine is usually too soft, but can be used. Oak and chestnut should be avoided because of their coarse texture and variable grain.

The steps followed in chip carving are shown in Fig. 1. The first step is to "stab" the design, as at A. A vertical cut is made with the skew knife, the toe of the knife being at the deepest part of the cut to be made. This point is the apex of the triangle, where the knife should go into the wood about ⅛ inch. The two sides of each triangle are stabbed in this manner, and the chip is then removed as shown at B. The knife may be held with the thumb resting firmly on the wood to serve as a base on which to pivot the hand while pushing the blade of the knife under the chip. Some carvers prefer to undercut the wood with a free hand, that is, without resting the thumb on the wood. Either method may be used, according to personal convenience and preference. When undercutting the chip in this way, the toe of the knife must be kept from going into the vertical walls made by the stabbing cuts, or into the adjoining chips. The completed cut and the cut-out chip are shown at C.

Small chips in straight-grained wood should be removed at one cut. Large or curved chips, or those in hard or crooked grain wood may require two or more cuts. You will quickly learn the best and most logical procedure once you begin to carve.

The heel of the skew knife or chisel, is generally used to make the

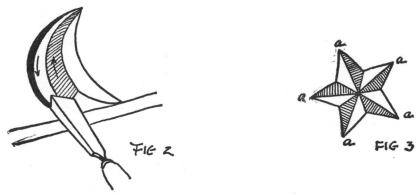

FIG 2

FIG 3

curved cuts, as shown in Fig. 2. Usually, when making cuts such as those shown in Fig. 2, the direction in which the cutting is done on one side will have to be reversed on the other side, as indicated by the arrows. The easiest and best way of handling such cuts under varying conditions will quickly be learned after a little practice.

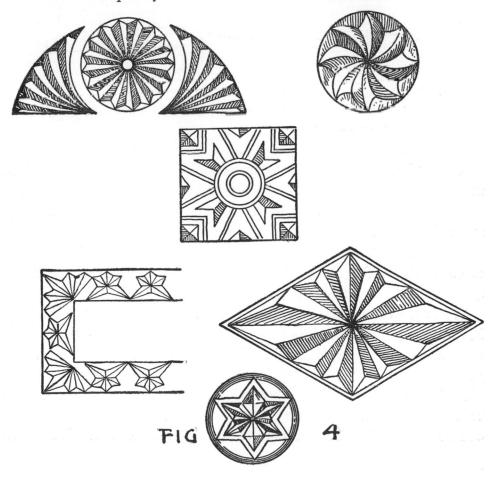

FIG 4

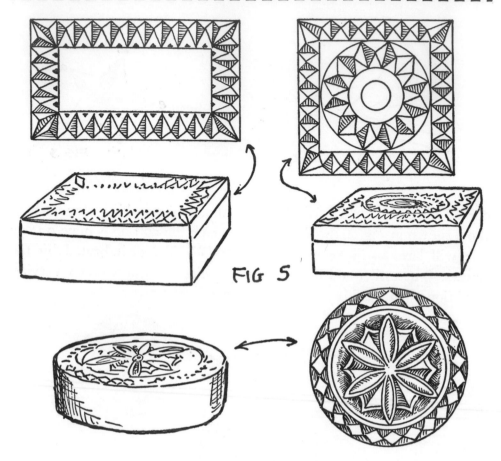

FIG 5

The design that you wish to carve should first be drawn on a piece of paper and then traced onto the wood by means of carbon paper.

Rectangular designs, some of which are shown in Fig. 4, are easily made. The outer lines of the design are first "stabbed" with the skew knife to make a vertical cut about ⅛ inch deep. The knife is then used to cut out a slanting indentation running from the surface of the wood down to the bottom of the vertical stabbing cut.

When the carving has been completed, the surface of the wood may be sandpapered, if needed; but care must be taken not to sandpaper and wear down the sharp edges and ridges of the cuts. Do not use sandpaper while doing the cutting, for this would dull your tools.

Articles decorated with chip carving are frequently given a wax or linseed oil finish. A wax finish is put on with commercial waxes which can be purchased at hardware or ten-cent stores. The wax is brushed

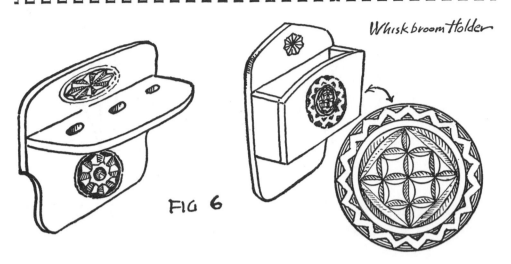

Whiskbroom Holder

FIG 6

on and then polished with a brush or piece of soft cloth. If linseed oil is used, there should be several applications, each rubbed well into the wood with a cloth. Each application should be allowed to dry thoroughly for several days before the next one is put on. Articles that are likely to be handled a good deal and therefore need cleaning from time to time are better finished with shellac or varnish.

To make a beginning at chip carving and get your hand in, start with a simple five-pointed star such as the one shown in Fig. 3. First draw a star on a piece of paper and transfer it to the wood by means of carbon paper. Each little triangle within the star is then cut out just as shown in Fig. 1. Each of the long radical lines, *a*, will then form an elevated ridge, from which the wood slopes away on each side toward the apexes of the two triangles of which each line *a* forms the dividing line.

Fig 7 - Photograph Frames — partly shown.

Book FIG 8 Ends

After carving a few stars, you will have learned the knack of chip carving and can practice on some of the more complicated designs shown in Fig. 4 and can then proceed to apply these and others designs to articles of the type shown in the succeeding drawings.

Figs. 5 to 9 give a number of suggestions for articles on which chip carving can be used to advantage, and an appropriate type of design is indicated for each one. The designs shown do not necessarily have to be used. Some of the articles shown such as the boxes, desk blotter,

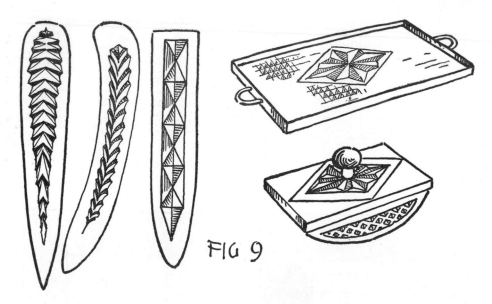

FIG 9

wastepaper basket and picture frames, can be purchased already made but in an unfinished state. Others, such as the pipe rack, whiskbroom holder, paper knives and tray can be easily made at a home work bench with a few tools—saw, plane, hammer and nails.

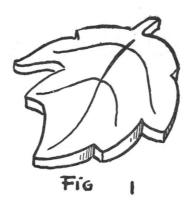

FIG 1

## INCISED CARVING

INCISING is the simplest form of wood carving, but one with which many beautiful and decorative affects may be obtained. In incised work, the design is formed by cutting out lines which have been drawn in pencil on the wood. (See Fig. 1.) After the design has been incised it may be stained in colors that contrast harmoniously with the background, which may be finished in a different color or a different tone of the same color.

When the lines of the design have been carved out, the background may be left plain or may be developed by threading-in (Fig. 2) or stippling (Fig. 3). The methods of doing these types of work are described later on in this chapter.

Learn at the beginning to work from one position and use your chisels and gouges to cut in any direction. Beginners sometimes form the habit of walking around their work, or continually shifting the position of the work on the bench. Do not do this. Experienced carvers stay in one position.

There are two ways in which the lines cut in the wood in this type of carving may be incised. One is to use a ⅛ or ¹⁄₁₆ inch veining tool, or if preferred a V-tool. The other is to use a hook-billed knife. In either case, it is best to clamp the wood in place so that it will not move while you are cutting the lines of the design.

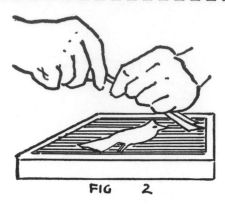

FIG 2

Fig. 2 shows how a veiner of V-tool is held when carving thin lines. The left hand holds the tool and guides it, while the right hand pushes it through the wood. When following the lines of the design drawn on the wood, the aim should be to make as continuous a line as possible without lifting the tool. When this is done, the finished effect is superior to that obtained by making a number of short cuts. Cut slowly while you are learning and try to keep each incised line constant in width.

When incising lines diagonally to the grain of the wood, one side of the tool will be cutting at an acute angle to the grain and will make a smooth cut. The other side, however, will be cutting at an obtuse angle, and may tear the wood. If the wood is torn, the incised line can be cleaned up by going over it in the opposite direction to the first cut. In making each cut press the tool toward the side of the line that

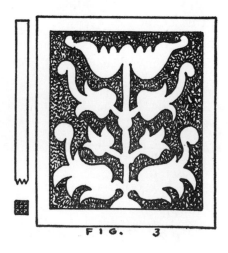

FIG. 3

meets the grain at an acute angle. Do not cut to the full depth on the first cut. Make a light marking cut first or draw a knife along the penciled line that is to be cut to serve as a guide for the veiner.

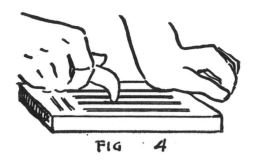

FIG 4

Fig. 4 shows how the hook-billed knife is held when doing incised carving. The knife is drawn along the penciled line and a cut about ¹⁄₁₆ inch deep is made right on the line. The knife is then slanted about 15 degrees and another cut is made just outside of the first line, that is, away from the inside of the design. This removes a small, almost hair-thin sliver of wood. This method of cutting is followed until all the lines of the design have been carved.

Sometimes carved wood is stained or painted all over. In other projects, a more striking effect can be obtained by staining only the lines that have been carved. When this is done, and the background wood is left plain, a water color stain should be used, rather than an oil stain, as the latter is apt to spread over the wood and spoil the clear-cut appearance of the carved lines.

Very often the background wood is decorated by threading-in or stippling. The threaded-in background is the one most commonly used and should be adopted in all work except that in which the design occupies so much space or is so complicated that threading-in is difficult or impossible.

Threading-in is usually done with a V-tool. Fig. 2 shows how the tool is controlled, and also shows a piece of work with a threaded-in background, which consists of a series of parallel lines. A stippled background (Fig. 3) is made with a metal punch of the type shown in Fig. 3. These may be purchased at wood or leathercraft supply stores or may be made from a piece of soft steel. When stippling a background, the punch should be turned to a different position after each stroke so as not to make its own pattern apparent.

When a background is threaded in or stippled, oil stains may be used over the entire surface of the wood. Since the background is rough, it will absorb more stain than the surface of the design, and the design will be several shades lighter, thus creating a two-tone effect. Two colors may also be used, one on the design and one on the background. The design can also be brought into prominence by rubbing its surface with fine steel wool after the stain has dried.

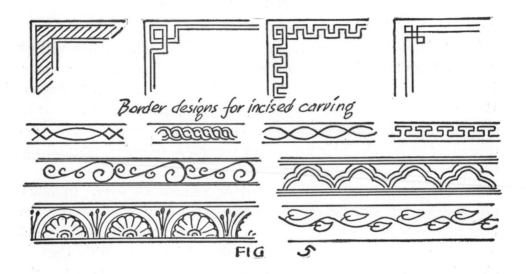

Border designs for incised carving

FIG 5

## DESIGNS AND PROJECTS FOR INCISED CARVING

Any of the common articles made of wood, such as boxes, book ends, decorative panels, picture frames, letter holders, desk blotter holders of the rocker type, bread trays and waste paper baskets, may be decorated with incised carving.

Before starting to carve an actual project, it will be a good idea to practice making a few designs on some odd piece of wood. Take a piece of soft wood, such as white pine, basswood or poplar, and carve some of the border designs shown in Fig. 5. Use a hook-billed knife or a veiner, whichever you prefer. Many of the other designs given in this book can be adapted to incised work. Fig. 6 shows some simple single-line designs that furnish additional ideas for incised carving. Designs such as these may be used for panel decorative or for any other surfaces which require decoration.

Designs for incised carving

FIG 6

Silhouette figures are frequently used in incised carving. If the background is threaded in or stippled, the entire piece of wood may be covered with an oil stain. The smooth silhouette will then show up several tones lighter than the roughened background. The two-tone effect can be accentuated by rubbing off some of the stain before it is dry, or by rubbing the surface of the silhouette when dry with fine steel wool. Instead of using an oil stain, the silhouette may be stained with an ebony stain or painted dull black and then rubbed to a smooth finish with fine steel wool. The background is then finished with a coat of light shellac, or stained with a very light tint.

Some suggested silhouette designs are shown in Fig. 7. They are **not** difficult to make, and other designs can be devised or copied from pictures in magazines or books. Profiles of members of the family, of friends or of well-known persons, make interesting silhouettes and are suitable for book ends, panels, and other gift articles. Initials and monograms are also excellent for silhouetted incised work.

Unlimited numbers of other designs for incised carving work can be found in illustrations in books and magazines. In choosing a design for a particular article, care should be taken to have it conform to the shape of the space that is to be decorated. Too much decoration should be avoided.

Fig. 8 shows a number of wooden articles decorated by means of easy-to-do incised carving. Directions for making each of these projects are not given in detail, since this is not a book on carpentry work. All of the articles are of very simple construction and can be made by anyone who is able to use a saw, hammer and nails, and other common tools. It is suggested, however, that if your primary interest is in wood carving and decorative work, rather than carpentry, that you purchase already-made undecorated wooden articles. This is what many wood carvers do. Many furniture stores, department stores, ten-cent stores and hardware stores have simply-made, undecorated wooden articles for sale, usually at relatively low prices. These include picture frames, magazine racks, letter holders, wooden boxes, book ends, small tables, bread boards, and a host of other useful things that are eminently suitable for wood carving. If you are fond of carpentry work and have a work

GIVE US
THIS DAY
OUR DAILY BREAD

FIG. 8.

bench and tools, you will probably want to make many of the articles that you subsequently decorate by carving. If, however, your chief interest is in carving, you will probably wish to buy wooden articles already made, but in an unfinished condition.

The incised work on the projects shown in Fig. 8 requires little explanation. In each case, the lines of the design or lettering are cut out by means of a hook-billed knife, or veiner or a V-tool. The designs can then be accentuated or brought out from the background by means of stains, as already described. All the articles shown can be obtained already made but in an unfinished condition, at the kinds of stores mentioned previously in this chapter.

FIG. 1

## CHASE CARVING

IN CHASE carving, the design is cut in the wood with a gouge, without working up the background to bring the work into relief. It is really another form of incising, and some craftsmen call it by that name. Chasing is a more commonly accepted name, however, and serves to distinguish this type of work from the simpler line cutting involved in incising.

The gouge is the most commonly used carving tool, and the execution of a few projects in chase carving will do much to familiarize the beginner with its use. For most chasing work, three gouges will be sufficient —the ⅛-inch, ¼-inch, and ⅜-inch, long-bend type.

Chasing is so simple to do that it requires but little explanation. Fig. 1 shows how the gouge is held and guided along the lines of the design, which have previously been marked in pencil on the surface of the wood. The right hand furnishes the motive power for the tool, and the left hand guides and controls it. Beginners should practice tracing curved and other lines on a spare piece of wood before commencing a finished project such as a pair of book ends, a box or a decorative panel.

Several articles decorated by means of chase carving are shown in Fig. 2. As can be seen, each design consists of lines or shapes cut into the wood with a gouge. This is easy-to-do work, but provides excellent practice in the handling of carving tools. Any of the articles shown on Page 97 can be decorated by means of chase carving by using designs that are suitable for gouge work. For the most part, such designs consist of straight or curved lines and oval leaf-like shapes. Circles can be

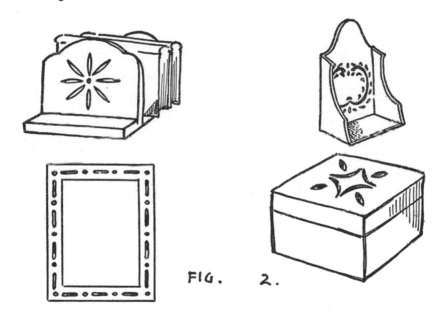

FIG. 2.

made by holding the gouge vertically above the wood and rotating the handle. This will cut a circle of the same shape as the gouge's cutting edge, and the wood inside it can then be split out with a knife.

Instructions for making numerous useful articles of this kind, the appearance of which can be immeasurably enhanced by chip carving or other carving, may be found in books on carpentry and wood-working which can be obtained at any medium-sized or large library. A number of books of this kind are listed in the Bibliography given in the back of this book.

A Lining in    FIG. 1     B Setting in     C Wasting away

## LEVEL SURFACE CARVING

The farther one goes with wood carving, the more absorbing the craft becomes and the greater the beauty of the articles that can be made. Beautiful and satisfying work can be executed by incising and chasing, but the effects obtainable by level-surface carving are richer and more artistic. This type of carving presents considerably more opportunity for ornamentation, and there is a wider range of designs that may be carved out. It is called level surface carving because the surface of the designs is flat, as contrasted to the rounded surfaces of carving modeled in relief.

It is wise for most beginners, however, to practice incising and chasing before attempting level surface carving. This is because the two former types of work develop skill in handling the various tools that will be of the greatest use when commencing level surface work.

In level surface or low relief carving, the design is on the surface of the wood and is brought into relief by cutting down the background, or spaces around the design. Frequently, a few added grooves are incised into the surface of the design with a veining tool to furnish accents and lines that make the design more effective or complete.

Five steps are usually followed in level surface carving. These are called (1) outlining, (2) lining in, (3) setting in, (4) wasting away, and (5) grounding out. (See Fig. 1.)

(1) After the pattern is drawn or traced on the wood with a pencil, it is outlined with a knife or a skew chisel held like a pencil. The tool is moved along the lines of the design to cut the wood fibers and make a path for the veiner to follow when lining in. The tool used for making

the outline cuts should be held so that it slants from the bottom of the cut outward. This makes a protecting edge for the relief design.

(2) Lining in is done with a veiner or parting tool, preferably the latter. One side of the tool's cutting edge follows the outline cut, and the other cuts out a V in the background or waste wood. (See A, Fig. 1.)

(3) In setting in, the short, straight lines of the design are cut with a chisel held vertically; and the quick or pronounced curves are cut by driving a gouge straight down into the wood. (See B, Fig. 1.) This operation separates the design from the surrounding background. If you are using soft wood, the tools are put in the V of the lining-in cut and pushed down into the wood a little more than 1/16 of an inch. If walnut or some other hard wood is being used, you will have to pound the handle of the tool with the palm of your hand; and with the harder woods, such as ebony, you will have to use the mallet.

When setting in concave curves with a gouge, use a gouge that is a trifle "quicker," or has a little more curve or "sweep," than the curve in the design. If this is done, the tips of the gouge will cut into the background wood, not into the design. Conversely, when setting in convex curves, use a gouge that is a little flatter than the curve of the design.

Be careful to make each setting-in cut connect with the preceding one. If you do not do this, the design will have saw-tooth edges. Always hold the tool you are using for setting in straight up and down. Otherwise you may undercut the design.

(4) Wasting away is the process of roughing out the wood from the background. (See C, Fig. 1.) It is usually done with quick gouges. Experienced carvers use the largest that they can get into the space being worked. The work should be done across the grain whenever possible, as the tool is then easier to control. After wasting away the large areas of the background with a large gouge, use smaller and flatter gouges for the corners and narrow places formed by the outlines of the design. When working into a corner, lift the gouge and turn it at the same time, using the lower tip as a pivot. This will enable you to cut out the background wood in the corner without splitting the wood forming the raised design.

(5) Grounding out is merely smoothing down the background with a chisel or a very flat gouge. The tool should be worked up carefully against the design. If, when grounding, you find that the setting-in cuts are not deep enough, make them a little deeper to get the required degree of relief.

In level surface carving, after the grounding is completed, the design looks as if it had been cut out of thin wood with a jigsaw and then glued onto the background. The background is rougher than the design itself and may be given a pattern with knife or chisel cuts. If the background is left with some roughness and tool marks, the effect is usually better than if an effort is made to smooth it out entirely. In some machine carving the background is decorated by means of punch marks, but experienced hand carvers avoid this method of decoration. Some, however, like to stipple in the background with a single stamp of the type shown in Fig. 3, Page 92 in order to obtain a rough mottled effect.

## DESIGNS AND PROJECTS FOR LEVEL SURFACE CARVING

When selecting designs for the level surface carving, choose those in which the parts of the design are not too small or delicate. Comparatively bold and simple figures, which fill the greater portion of the space to be carved, are desirable. A number of designs are illustrated in the present chapter, but they are only a fraction of those that are available. Suggestions can be found in dozens of places, such as rugs, textile fabrics, pictures and advertisements in books and magazines, and in special books on design, some of which are available at almost every public library.

Figs. 2 and 3 show a number of designs that are suitable for level surface carving. These can be adapted to any of the articles already illustrated and to many others. This type of carving, moreover, is frequently used for decorating pieces of furniture, such as tables, chairs, footstools and book cases. Inexpensive unfinished pieces of furniture can be purchased and decorated with really beautiful designs of the kinds shown in Fig. 2 even by beginners at wood carving. When carved and stained, the finished articles will make gifts of enduring

FIG. 2

loveliness and value. Unfinished furniture is largely made of pine and other soft woods, but it is wise to find out just what kind of wood has been used. There is a possibility that you might encounter some of the hard woods and would not want to carve these till you are a more experienced carver. Wooden panels carved with some of the designs shown and stained in harmonious or contrasting colors make gifts that are very much out of the ordinary, which are sure to be treasured by those who receive them. Level surface carving lends itself particularly well to striking color schemes, and the finished effect of the carving is frequently very much enhanced by the use of well-chosen colors.

Start your level carving work by working up some of the designs shown in Figs. 2 and 3 on practice pieces of wood. When you have gained a little experience in this way, you can carve designs on boxes, frames, gift panels, and other useful articles.

The border designs shown in Fig. 2 can be used for picture frames, mirror frames, wooden boxes, furniture, and a host of other wooden articles. The patterns shown in Fig. 3 can be used for the same types of articles to decorate central spaces and flat surfaces.

FIG. 3

While the designs in level surface carving are usually perfectly flat, it is sometimes possible to give them a little modeling by making it appear that certain parts of the design overlap others. This effect can be seen in several of the border designs shown in Fig. 2 in which the pattern consists of interlaced ribbons. One ribbon is made to appear to pass under another by lowering the level of the wood at the point where

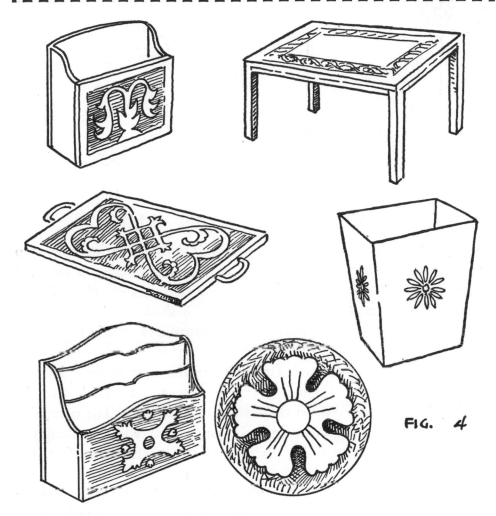

FIG. 4

the two ribbons meet. This is done by making a stop-cut at the edge of the ribbon on top and then slicing a thin wedge from the ribbon that passes beneath.

Several of the patterns shown in Figs. 2 and 3 are shown as carved work on various wooden articles in Fig. 4. For other suggested articles, see Page 81.

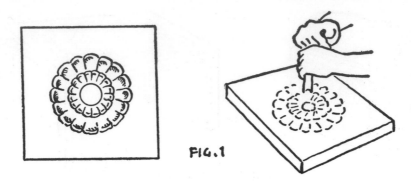

FIG. 1

## CARVING MODELED IN RELIEF

CARVING modeled in relief carries level surface carving one step farther, for it is level surface carving in which the design is rounded and modeled by means of gouges, chisels, and fluting tools. (See Fig. 1.) Modeled carving adds the values of light and shade to the work, and creates sculptured forms that are more beautiful and artistic than those which have a flat or level surface.

The first steps in model relief carving are the same as those in level surface carving. The design is drawn on paper and traced onto the wood or is drawn directly on the surface of the wood. The successive steps of outlining, lining in, setting in, wasting away and grounding out are then carried out to bring the design into relief. Thereafter, the design is modeled.

An example, such as the rosette shown in Fig. 1 will make clear the methods and tools used for modeling work. After the rosette has been brought into relief as in level surface carving, the petals are hollowed out with gouges, the width and sweep of the gouge conforming to the size of the petals. The same method is used here as in cutting down the background—the same rule holds good—namely, waste the wood away slowly, a little at a time. A smaller gouge is needed for the inner petals, for example, than for the larger outside ones. To round the circle in the center of the rosette, use a gouge which exactly fits the curve of the circle, and make a deep, vertical stop—cut all around it. Then, turning the gouge face downward, slice with a curving stroke from the center of the circle downward and outward, taking off a thin slice with each stroke. Continue slicing until the circle is rounded off and appears like a small sphere sunken in the wood. You will have to make rounded shapes of this type frequently, as they are extensively used in wood-carving designs. They are known as "pearls."

Many uses may be found for a carving of this kind. It can be used for the lid of a box, on book ends, on the door of a cabinet, on the top of a small table, and on many other wooden articles.

FIG. 2

Another design that can be used for many purposes is shown in Fig. 2. The large leaves are modeled with a very flat gouge, and the small work in the center is done with a narrow gouge having a quick or well-rounded sweep. The "in-lines" in the design, meaning the central veins of the leaves which are entirely within the design, are made with a $\frac{1}{16}$-inch veiner.

Fig. 3 shows the three stages involved in modeling a cartouche, which is a little more difficult than the previously described designs. For the cartouche you must be sure to select a piece of wood thick enough to permit deep carving, as the scrolls of the design will project $\frac{1}{4}$ inch or more above the background.

Draw or trace the outline of the design in the surface of the wood, and then bring the cartouche into $\frac{1}{4}$-inch relief, as already described under "Level Surface Carving." Mark in pencil outlines of the scrolls

A      B    FIG. 3     C

or parts where the edges curl inward. Then, with a flat gouge, waste away the remainder of the cartouche, working it down until it is about ⅟₁₆ inch in depth. The carving will then appear as at A. Note that the surface of the cartouche is not flat, but is hollowed out so that the central part is lower than the edges. This done by slicing downward toward the center from all sides with a flat gouge.

Next trace the outline of the oval shape in the center of the cartouche and round its surface as though it were a "pearl," following the directions given above for Fig. 1. The three scrolls are then rounded by means of flat gouges and the modeling is completed by adding the various "in-lines" shown at C by means of a veiner. When the cartouche is finished, it may be painted in contrasting colors, and the panel can be framed by moulding.

There is nearly no end to the designs and patterns that can be discovered for carving modeled in relief, once you have projects under way and begin to look about you for suitable design material. There are infinite varieties of leaf and flower designs alone, and with the addition of animal and human forms and natural and artificial objects of different kinds, you will find an abundance of material from which to choose. Pictures in books and magazines will provide ideas or suggestions. Panels can be made showing scenes from fairy stories, the Mother Goose rhymes, or from the Bible. Fig. 4 shows a number of motives and patterns that are favorites with wood carvers and can be used for various projects.

The "Tudor rose" in Fig. 4 may be used as a good illustration of the steps to be followed in carving and modeling the many floral figures of similar type that are widely used in wood carving. The first step is to indicate the principal parts of the figure by means of pencil lines drawn

TUDOR ROSE

FIG. 4

on the wood or traced onto the wood from a drawing made on paper. Start with a square piece of wood, and then, after the carving is under-way, cut away the corners to make it circular. When completed, the rose is glued or cemented to a background piece of wood.

Draw four concentric circles to indicate the outer edges of the large and small petals and the central "pearl," and straight radial lines to show the lines of division between the petals.

When starting to carve, first outline the pearl and set in about ⅜ inch. Use a chisel or flat gouge and make sloping cuts downward from the inner petals to the ⅜-inch deep setting-in cut around the pearl. Draw in the outlines of the large and small petal tops in pencil and also the tri-angular leaves between them. Then carve the large petals to shape, using a gouge and wasting away the wood little by little. Carve down-ward toward the inner petals. Next shape up the curved sides of the large outer petals and the triangular leaves between them. Waste away the inner petals and cut the grooves between them with a veiner. Then round up the pearl, as already described, and complete the carving by making the grooves across the pearl and the three little marks in each inner petal with a veiner. Five small holes are added with a punch or a

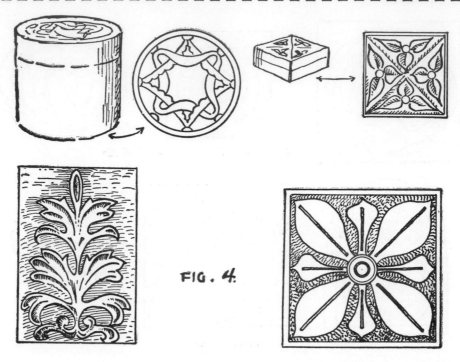

FIG. 4.

very small gouge at the points where the edges of the inner petals meet the pearl.

A little practice at carving the designs described will do wonders toward giving you the "feel" of the various tools and in creating confidence in your ability. As many a beginner has discovered after he has tried his hand at a few modeled designs such as those shown in Fig. 4, wood carving is not nearly as difficult as it is sometimes believed to be.

# BIBLIOGRAPHY

*Books that tell how to make furniture and other articles
that can be decorated by carving*

Adams, J. T. and Stieri, E., *The Complete Woodworking Handbook;* Arco, 1960

D'Amico, V. and others, *How to Make Objects of Wood;* Simon and Schuster, 1952

Durst, A., *Wood Carving;* Viking, 1959

Gottshall, F. H., *Woodwork for the Beginner;* Bruce, 1952

Gross, F., *How to Work with Tools and Wood;* Pocket Books

Hamilton, E. T., *Home Carpentry;* Dodd, Mead, 1940

Hayward, C. H., *Carpentry for Beginners,* Lippincott, 1951

Hayward, C. H., *Junior Woodworker;* Lippincott, 1952

Home Craftsman, *Home Woodwork Projects*

Home Mechanics Library, *Carpentry and Woodworking;* Van Nostrand

Hooper, J., *Handcraft in Wood;* Lippincott, 1953

Hunt, W. B., *Whittling with Ben Hunt;* Bruce, 1959

Lewis, R., *Woodworking;* Knopf, 1952

Popular Mechanics, *The Boy Mechanic;* Golden Press, 1952

Pynn, L., Jr., *Let's Whittle;* Bennett, 1948

Shea, J. G., *Woodworking for Everybody;* Van Nostrand

Upton, J., *Art of Woodcarving;* Van Nostrand, 1958